HINDU VIEW OF CHRISTIANITY AND ISLAM

HINDU VIEW OF CHRISTIANITY AND ISLAM

RAM SWARUP

VOICE OF INDIA
New Delhi

First published 1992
Fifth reprint 2019

ISBN 978-81-85990-66-8

Website: www.voiceofin.com

Published by Voice of India, 2/18, Ansari Road, New Delhi – 110 002.
Printed at Replika Press Pvt. Ltd.

Dedicated to

HARI PRASAD LOHIA
(April 14, 1923 - October 15, 1992)

who played a noble part
in a common endeavour and seeking,
who shared the idea of this book, and
who had a role in the making and shaping of
Voice of India

CONTENTS

PREFACE

Hindu View of Christianity and Islam is a sequel to *Hinduism vis-a-vis Christianity and Islam* which was recently issued in a new, enlarged edition.

The first two chapters of this volume reproduce two Introductions which we wrote for the Indian Reprints of two Lives of Muhammad, both classics, one written by Professor D.S. Margoliouth in 1900, and the other even earlier by Sir William Muir. Both were pioneer studies and both are still unequalled in the treatment of the subject. As a study of Muhammad is at bottom also a study of Islam, both were also excellent studies of the creed the prophet inaugurated.

But both had also one common failing; they studied the subject from a Western-Christian viewpoint, Muir consciously and frankly so; they neglected the pagan viewpoint including that of Arabia, the immediate victim of the new ideology. The purpose of the Introductions was to remove or, at least, to draw attention to this lacuna while Hindus made use of Western-Christian scholarship in the absence of their own. In the Introductions, we also tried to look at Christianity and Islam through the viewpoint of larger paganism and discuss them in the larger Hindu spiritual framework. As a result, these Introductions acquired an unusual interest; we are therefore reproducing them here.

The third chapter carries forward the discussion still further. It elaborates certain points only briefly mentioned before and discusses new ones providing fresh viewpoints and additional information. It discusses Messiahs, Saviours and Prophets; it discusses the ideology of iconoclasm, missions and *jihād*; it discusses prophetic and yogic spiritualities; it discusses yogic and non-yogic *samādhis* and how the two project their own respective revelations, Gods and ethical codes. It discusses the prophetic god and revelation in the light of the Yoga.

Though Christianity has a poor opinion of Islam, yet it

regards it as a partner up to a point; it welcomes Islam's role as a cleanser of the "world from the gross pollution of idolatry," — the name by which the two religions remember all other religions, past or present. This sympathy arises from the fact that the two religions in spite of a long history of conflicts share a common perspective and common ideological premises.

In their career, the two ideologies have been active and systematic persecutors of pagan nations, cultures and religions; but the histories of the victims have been written from the victors' viewpoint, and their viewpoint has prevailed in judging the victims. Here, we have not accepted the victors' standard of judgement; on the other hand, we have tried to look at them from the viewpoint of paganism in general and of Hindu spirituality in particular. We have spoken here with sympathy and respect not only of pagan Americas and Africa but also of the pagan past of Egypt, Greece Rome, Europe, Iran, Syria and old Arabia. This itself is unusual considering that their images have been thoroughly blackened, thanks to the triumph of monolatrous religions which vilify their neighbours as well as their own ancestors. But this has to go. A truly growing humanity cannot live with such a blackened past. Its past must be as glorious as it expects its future to be.

Today, there is a new awakening in many parts of the world. Many peoples are coming to know what they have gone through and how much they have lost. They have also begun to realize that their present religions are impositions on them, that they once belonged to a different spiritual culture which had a different orientation and was built on a deeper and a wider base. As this realization becomes more acute, many of them are trying to break from their present confines and are trying to recover their lost identity. They are also seeking a more satisfying spirituality. Probably Hinduism can help them. It has itself survived many physical and ideological onslaughts and it still retains in its bosom layers of spiritual traditions, intuitions and knowledge which other nations have lost; it can, therefore, help these nations to recover their lost religious roots and identity.

Hinduism-Buddhism represents not only man's continuity

with his past but also the innermost truth of his soul. It is a most complete statement and formulation available of *philosophia perennis*, Perennial Philosophy, the *Sanātana Dharma*. It can, therefore, also meet man's seeking for a deeper religion.

Navarātra, Āśvin Śukla Pratipadā
September 27, 1992

RAM SWARUP

ONE

CHRISTIANITY AND ISLAM: DOCTRINAL AFFINITY BUT HISTORICAL CONFLICT*

Oriental Studies in the West has a long history. It has its genesis in the Christian–Muslim encounter. From its very birth, Islam found itself in conflict with neighbouring Christianity. Moved by the same passion and making the same claim, the two religions engaged in bitter strife for a thousand years. Islam knocked at the doors of Christianity, overwhelming much of Europe for centuries. Eventually Christianity replied with the sword of the crusades. The tide of Islam was stemmed; Western Christianity was united; the power of the Pope increased tremendously; and Western Christianity became East-oriented. The East became an object of a continuous aggressive quest.

The armed crusades themselves ended in ignominy by the end of the thirteenth century. Christianity now thought of other means of penetration. As Waddington puts it in his *History of the Church*, when "the arms of the Mohammedan were found to preponderate, some faint attempts were made, or meditated, to convince those whom it proved impossible to subdue." As a first step, Pope Honorius IV (AD 1286–1287) encouraged the study of oriental languages as an aid to missionary work. Soon after, the Ecumenical Council of Vienna (AD 1311–1312) decided "that the holy Church should have an abundant number of Catholics well versed in the languages, especially in those of the infidels, so as to be able to instruct them in the sacred doctrine." Therefore, it ordered the creation of chairs of Hebrew, Arabic, and Chaldaean at the Universities of Bologna, Oxford, Paris, and Salamanca.

How far this decree was immediately implemented is not known but the strategic importance of Oriental Studies was clearly established. After another hundred years, the General

* Introduction to the reprint of *Mohammed and the Rise of Islam* by D.S. Margoliouth.

Council of Basel (AD 1434) returned to the same theme and decreed that "all Bishops must sometimes each year send some men well-grounded in the divine word to those parts where Jews and other infidels live, to preach and explain the truth of the Catholic faith in such a way that the infidels who hear them may come to recognise their errors. Let them compel them to hear their preaching."

But for the next several generations, the Church had to train for polemics within its own fold. It faced internal revolts. Strong Protestant movements came to the fore, questioning several Catholic dogmas and the Pope's authority. These made big holes in the citadel of the Church. All this was uncomfortable for the time being, but eventually it did good to Christianity as a whole. Through "challenge-and-response" it made it battle-ready. And though different Christian groups had acute internal quarrels, they all faced the non-Christian world unitedly. After a lull, the Protestant nations too joined the missionary game with great fervour. In fact, considering themselves as the rightful heirs to true Christianity, they were sure they would succeed where the Catholic Church had failed. According to them, the Romish Church—the Protestant name for Catholics—was bound to fail, choked as it was with its own errors. George Sale, the first European to produce a faithful translation of the Quran, wrote in 1734 that "the Protestants alone are able to attack the Koran with success"; and in fact, it is for them that "Providence has reserved the glory of its overthrow." More than a hundred years later, Sir William Muir, a representative of the mighty British Empire, expressed the same sentiment. He asked the question why the Muslim world was not already converted, considering the fact that the banners of Islam had approached so closely the Papal See. His answer was that "the bigotry of the Mussulmans, the licence of concubinage and slavery, and their otherwise low standard of morality" only partly explained this failure on the part of Christianity. The other part of the explanation was the superstitious practices of the Church itself which "froze the current, which should have flowed unceasingly, diffusing to the nations around the genial and healing streams of Christianity"

(*Calcutta Review*, 1845).

It was against this background that the Christian researchers began their study of Islam. These early studies did little to improve their opinion of the rival creed. They regarded it as a "spurious faith" and its author as a "false prophet," an opinion which has not fundamentally changed since then though it is no longer stated with the same candour as in the past.

Within the framework of this hostile opinion, some concession began to be made in due course. Islam was evil but its role in destroying idolatry with a strong hand was praiseworthy. For example, Rev. Charles Forster, a clergyman of the Church of England, and author of *Mohammedanism Unveiled* (1829), regarded Islam as a "baleful superstition," and its founder an "impostor, earthly, sensual, devilish, beyond even the licence of his licentious creed," but he still regarded this creed as "confessedly superior" to the gross idolatry of its predecessor. Islam has a place in the divine scheme. Considered in itself, and as opposed to the Gospel, it is a "curse"; but as the "pre-appointed scourge of heresy and heathenism, as cleansing the world from the gross pollutions of idolatry, and preparing the way for the reception of a purer faith [Christianity], it may well be regarded as a blessing."

Like Marx who hated Capitalism but regarded it as a higher form of economic and political organisation and welcomed capitalists as sappers and miners of Communism, Christianity detested Islam but honoured it for destroying idolatry.

However, even this approach was considered too hostile and there were thinkers from an early date who canvassed for a still more liberal treatment of Islam. George Sale whom we have already mentioned pleaded that "how criminal soever Mohammed may have been in imposing a false religion on mankind, the praises due to his real virtues ought not to be denied him." Were not the laws he gave to his people "preferable, at least, to those of the ancient pagan lawgivers?" And therefore, did he not deserve, Sale asked, at least equal respect, "though not with Moses or Jesus Christ, whose laws came really from Heaven, yet with Minos and Numa ?"— the religious legislators of ancient Crete and Rome. Sale quoted with approval the example of the pious and learned Spanhemius who though he regarded Muhammad as a "wicked impostor" yet acknowledged his natural endowments, his subtle wit, his agreeable behaviour, his liberality and courtesy, his fortitude against his enemies, and above all his reverence for the name of God.

As the translations of the Quran became available, some Christian writers began dimly to perceive that Muhammad's virtues and vices were not his own but that he shared them with Biblical prophets. But these Christian writers were taught to castigate in the Quran what they had been taught to admire in the Bible. How could they do it consistently and conscientiously ? They found that some of the cruelest and fanatical passages in the Quran—like "kill them wherever ye find them" (2.191)—had a solid Biblical support and precedent. Rev. E.M. Wherry states this predicament in his *A Comprehensive Commentary on Quran* (1882). Referring to this injunction, *kill them*, he says: "Much is made of expressions like this, by some Christian apologists, to show the cruel character of the Arabian prophet, and the inference is thence drawn that Muhammad was an impostor and his Quran a fraud. Without denying that Muhammad was cruel, we think this mode of assault to be very unsatisfactory to say the least, as it is capable of being turned against the Old Testament Scriptures. If the claim of Muhammad to have received a divine command to exterminate idolatry by the slaughter of all impenitent idolaters be admitted, I can see no objection to his practice. The question at issue is this, Did God command such slaughter of idolaters, as he commanded the destruction of the Canaanites or of the Amalekites [Deut. 7.1, 2; Joshua 6.21, 24] ? Taking the stand of the Muslim, that God did so command Muhammad and his followers, his morality in this respect may be defended on precisely the same ground that the morality of Moses and Joshua is defended by the Christians" (Volume I, p. 358).

The fact is that while the Christian writers used strong adjectives and hurled hostile epithets, they had no proper grounds for attack. Some of the more perceptive ones among them probably even realized that an attack on Islam in a fundamental way was an attack on Christianity itself, since the two were so similar in their source, deeper perspective and psychic affinity. Both derived from a common source in the Old Testament; both were monolatrous; both claimed to be God's chosen fraternities; in both, God–man communication took place through a favoured intermediary; both had human founders; both were credal religions.

But all this similarity failed to bring them together. On the contrary, this made Islam into an "undisguised and formidable antagonist." William Muir puts it bluntly: "From all the varieties of heathen religions Christianity has nothing to fear for they are but the passive exhibitions of gross darkness which must vanish before the light of the Gospel. But in Islam we have an active and powerful enemy;—a subtle usurper, who has climbed into the throne under pretence of legitimate succession; and seized upon the forces of the crown to supplant its authority. It is just because Mohammedanism acknowledges the divine original, and has borrowed so many of the weapons of Christianity, that it is so dangerous an adversary."

The true cause of the conflict is of course different from the one imagined here by Muir. It consists in an inadequate conception of the Godhead on the part of both Christianity and Islam. The God of both teaches them to persecute religions other than their own; both are dogmatic, fundamentalist and theological; both lack Yoga or a proper science or discipline of inner exploration; both seek outward expansion; both are aggressively self-righteous; and both by nature know no true theory of peaceful co-existence.

India along with Egypt, Persia and Syria offered fertile opportunities for Christian Arabists and researchers in Islam. Henry Martyn, a Cambridge scholar with a flair for languages, came to India as a Chaplain in 1806 and joined the notorious William Carey group. He completed a version of the New Testament in Urdu and carried through a thorough revision of a Persian one. He also carried on theological controversies in the Persian language with the Muslim Divines of Persia. Rev. C.G. Pfander, first attached to the German Mission, later joined the

Indian Mission of C.M.S. in 1838. He wrote several polemical works in Persian: *Mīzān-ul-Haqq* (Balance of Truth); *Tariq-ul-Hayāt* (Way of Salvation: A Treatise on Sin and Redemption); *Miftah-ul-Asrār* (Key of Mysteries: A Treatise on the Divinity of Christ and the Doctrine of the Holy Trinity). A. Sprenger spent a great part of his life in India in search of material for the history of early Islam. It was in India that Waqidi, a very early, authoritative and orthodox biography of Muhammad, was discovered by him. In 1865, he brought out *The Life and Doctrine of Mahomet from Sources hitherto for the most part Unused;* twenty years earlier, he had published a *Life of Mohammed* from Allahabad.

But of this genera of writing, William Muir's *The Life of Mahomet*, first published in 1861 in four volumes, was the best. It was a pioneering study and it has not been improved upon since then. William Muir had strong Christian views but he was also a painstaking and conscientious researcher, and he exhausted most of the sources on the Prophet's life, which were not many. The basic material on Muhammad is limited and new biographies could not really be new except in details, treatment and emphases.

In fact, in most biographies except the hagiographical ones in which miracles abound, there is a remarkable agreement on *facts*, though the biographers differ in the way they look at those facts. For example, take the case of the Jewish tribe of Banu Quraiza whose people were massacred by the Prophet when they surrendered to him. The earliest Muslim biographers of impeccable orthodoxy celebrate the event with undisguised glee. The fashion to appear better than one is, a Christian innovation, was not in the early Muslim style. The Christian writers of the last century like Sprenger, Muir, Gustav Weil, Osborn, finding in the event an opportunity of attacking a rival creed, treated it with moral horror. But by the time Dr. David Samuel Margoliouth was writing in the beginning of this century, the moral horror was considerably subdued; so he simply narrates the event as a matter of fact. He also observes that we must try "in estimating this matter, to think of bloodshed as the Arabs thought of it: as an act which involves no stigma on the shedder." This was bad history and was unfair to the pre-Muslim Arabs, but it agreed with the new intellectual fashion. Ever since Margoliouth's times, things have moved still further in the same direction. Maxime Rodinson, a distinguished French Arabist, writing his *Mohammed* in the sixties of this century finds that Muhammad had his compulsions and "from a purely political point of view, moreover, the massacre was an extremely wise move"; and again that "the chosen solution was undeniably the best."

In this connection, we need not reproduce the elaborate apology which Syed Ameer Ali provides from the viewpoint of a modern Muslim apologist. To him, the punishment of the Jews was self-invited and they were self-condemned. He also shows with the help of many citations from Christian scriptures and history that this "defensive" massacre, in all its fearfulness and gruesomeness, was nothing compared to similar things we find in the Bible and in the history of Christianity. Read, for example, II Samuel 8.1-5 of the Bible.

II

We have observed that missionary consideration provided the initial impulse and also a continuing motive for the study of Islam. But in due course of time, as a result of many developments, the religious factor became less pronounced and also less important. One reason was that another motive, the imperial motive, was coming to the fore. Sometimes it reinforced the missionary motive but on many occasions it also opposed it. Another reason was that Europe was undergoing a rationalist revolution. Religion, as Europe knew it, was becoming suspect. Christianity felt less self-confident and won less sympathy for its viewpoint. The third reason had to do with the nature of the new scholarship itself. Though it started in a Christian motivation, in due course, it acquired its own independent dimension. Its inner dynamism and internal discipline carried it beyond its early confines. Once the Muslim classics were unearthed and texts edited, they became available for larger inspection; they could not be put to one, single, pre-arranged use.

All these factors had become important when Margoliouth wrote his *Mohammed*. Margoliouth was a great linguist and scholar and was for a long time a professor of Arabic at the University of Oxford. He wanted his book neither to be an indictment nor an apology, and he did not fail in this endeavour. He was writing for a "tolerant" twentieth-century audience and he decided, even before he wrote his book, to observe towards the prophet "the respectful attitude which his greatness deserves"; and even though the facts he cites sometimes do not do credit to his conclusion, in this resolve too he succeeded .

Margoliouth was also a minister of the Church of England, but he wanted his book to be "absolutely free" from the Christian bias; here too one can safely say that his book shows no conscious Christian bias. If a bias has to be mentioned, it is a European's imperial bias which regards all non-European manners and institutions—in this particular case, Bedouin manners and institutions—as savage.

Margoliouth went over all the old sources again and took into account all the fresh material that became available, but as we have already observed, a new biographer, even with the near-legendary reputation of Margoliouth, had little substantially new to add. He could only weave old facts differently and add fresh information or insight or speculation here and there, which he does with credit and distinction. In this spirit, Margoliouth offers an interesting theory that Islam began as a "secret society," and that secrecy added to its appeal initially. He also tells us an interesting fact that the word *muslim* etymologically means a *traitor*, and that the word was so used originally for the adherents of Islam by its opponents. The word initially signified one who handed over his friends to their enemies—a reference to Islam's early "connections" with Abyssinia, Mecca's "national" enemy—but Muhammad cleverly gave the word a dignified meaning of one who handed over his person to Allah. There is nothing strange in this fact. History is full of instances where derogatory epithets become proud titles.

Like so many other biographers of Muhammad, Margoliouth too was intrigued by his revelations, and he tries to understand them. The subject is difficult and also delicate but the author tackles it with ability and tact. He regards many explanations except the traditional Muslim one which holds God or Gabriel as their author. The new intellectual climate is against such a view, and it is clear that the author finds the whole process of revelations "suspicious." Nothing conclusive is said but several hypotheses are hinted at including the medical one of "epileptic fits" and the moral one of "trickery." A sociological view is also taken. Some hold that Muhammad's apostleship was accepted because the Arabs of his times were expecting a prophet of their own. This may be true but it does not explain why Muhammad alone should have met the expectation; nor is there much evidence that his countrymen were feeling particularly "desolate at the want of a prophet," as Margoliouth observes.

He also perceives behind these revelations a deep and steady motive of "personal distinction" on the part of Muhammad. Probably he was a character in search of a role and he wanted to reproduce in himself "the role of Moses and Jesus." Muhammad's revelations had two dogmas: (1) the dogma of *One God* which he borrowed from the Bible, and (2) the dogma of his own apostleship, which is his specific contribution. As Margoliouth observes, "the second was the dogma to which he [Muhammad] attached the greater importance." In fact, this was the "fundamental dogma of his system; agreement on other points presently became useless, if that were not conceded," the author observes.

Some biographers of Muhammad have held that his revelations were an imposture and their pretender was insincere. Margoliouth does not discuss the question on this level at all, and dodges it altogether by holding that "to those who are studying merely the political effectiveness of supernatural revelations, the sincerity of the medium is a question of little consequence."

For more light on the subject, the author also took the help of the science of *Spiritualism* (the alleged calling up of the departed spirits through a sensitive medium) of his days. With its help, he came to believe that Muhammad's revelations were "mediumistic communications." In *Spiritualism*, the problem of a medium is to produce a trustworthy revelation or a revelation which would be regarded as such. Muhammad faced a similar problem and he solved it in a similar way. Margoliouth also observes that like the medium, Muhammad enjoyed also a similar advantage: the medium is helped by the fact that the "conviction produced by the performances of a medium is often not shaken by the clearest exposure."

The author also sees a family likeness between the Muslim prophet and the prophet of the Mormons, Joseph Smith (1805–1844), and their respective revelations. It is true that Mormonism and Islam, and for that matter also other creeds like Bahaism (named after Baha-ul-lah, 1817–1892), and Babism (faith of Mirza Ali Muhammad, 1819–1850), are close cousins. But Muhammad started no new fashion. He himself followed an old model very well established in the Bible. Indeed to raise deeper questions about Muhammad's revelations is to raise questions about the whole species of revelatory spirituality of which the Bible is the scripture *par excellence*. This Margoliouth was not taught to do, nor was it a part of his seeking. In fact, this fundamental question has rarely been raised.

The spiritual equipage of Islam and Christianity is similar; their spiritual contents, both in quality and quantum, are about the same. The central piece of the two creeds is "one true God" of masculine gender who makes himself known to his believers through an equally single, favoured individual. The theory of mediumistic communication has not only a psychology; it has also a theology laid down long ago in the oldest part of the Bible in Deuteronomy (18.19, 20). The biblical God says that he will speak to his chosen people through his chosen prophet: "I will tell him what to say, and he will tell the people everything I command. He will speak in my name, and I will punish anyone who refuses to obey him" *(Good News Bible)*.

The whole prophetic spirituality, whether found in the Bible or in the Quran, is mediumistic in essence. Here everything takes place through a proxy, through an intermediary. Here man knows God through a proxy; and probably God too knows man through the same proxy. The proxy is the favoured individual, a privileged mediator. "No one knows the Son except the Father, and no one knows the Father except the Son and anyone to whom the Son chooses to reveal him," says the Bible (Mt. XI. 27). The Quran makes no very different claim. "This day have I perfected your religion for you," says the Allah of the Quran through his last prophet (5.3).

There are other similarities of the same fundamental kind into which we need not go here. But none of them are calculated to promote peace. The seeds of conflict, not only amongst the "believers" but also with the rest of the world, lie at the very heart of the two ideologies. Each of the two is presided over by a bellicose God, each chief of his own hosts; each claims sole sovereignty. A larger charity and mutual respect and even tolerance, and co-existence cannot be the strong points of such theologies.

III

Like Christianity, Hinduism too, though not by its own choice, found itself in conflict with Islam. But unlike the former, it never tried to study it. Hindus fought Muslim invaders and locally established Muslim dynasties but neglected to study the religious and ideological motives of the invaders. Hindu learning, or whatever remained of its earlier glory, followed the old grooves and its texts and speculations remained unmindful of the new phenomenon in their midst. For example, even as late as the thirteenth century, when Malik Kafur was attacking areas in the far South, in the vicinity of the seat of Sri Ramanujacharya, the scholarly dissertations of the disciples of the great teacher show no awareness of this fact.

Hindus were masters of many spiritual disciplines; they had many Yogas and they had a developed science of inner exploration. There had been a continuing discussion whether the ultimate reality was *dvaita* or *advaita*. It would have been very interesting and instructive to find out if any of these savants of Yoga ever met, on their inner journey, a Quranic being, Allah (or its original, Jehovah of the Bible), who is jealous of other

Gods, who claims sole sovereignty and yet whom no one knows except through a pet go-between, who appoints a favourite emissary and uses the latter's mouth to publish his decrees, who proclaims crusades and *jihād,* who teaches to kill the unbelievers and to destroy their shrines and temples, and to levy permanent tribute on them, and to convert them into *zimmīs,* into hewers of wood and drawers of water. Even today, the question retains its importance. Is the Allah of the Quran a spiritual being? Or, is he some sort of a mental and vital formation, a hegemonic idea? Does he represent man's own deepest truth and reside in his innermost being ? Or, is he a projection of a less edifying source in man's psyche? Is he discovered when a man's heart is tranquil, desireless and pure? Or, does he originate in a fevered state of the mind? Is his source the *samādhi* of the *yoga-bhūmi,* or some sort of a trance of a non-yogic *bhūmi*? In the *Yogadarshana,* this distinction is fundamental but it is not much remembered these days.

What is the truth of Prophetism which lays down that God can be known only indirectly through a favourite intermediary, a 'Sole Begotten Son' or a 'Last Prophet'? Even today these and other allied questions seek elucidation but Hindu spirituality remains silent. Is it because the Hindu spirit has been overtaken by *tamas,* inertia, and therefore remains slothfully neglectful? Or, does it inhabit a region which is beyond the storms and blasts of passing creeds and ideological fashions? Is it in a state, as has been said, which lets the legions thunder past and plunges in deep contemplation of the eternal verities again? Or, is the silence only seeming and it already contains a deep answer for those who have eyes to see and ears to hear?

Indian spirituality did not argue, debate or oppose. But did it not provide a complete answer ? It proclaimed that the true Godhead was beyond number and count; that it had many manifestations which did not exclude or repel each other but included each other and went together in friendship; that it was approached in different ways and through many symbols; that it resided in the heart of its devotees. Here there were no chosen peoples, no exclusive prophethoods, no privileged churches and fraternities and *ummahs*. The message was subversive of all religions based on exclusive claims.

Moreover, creeds like Christianity and Islam were not wholly unexpected by the Indian sages. Religions of exteriority like these had to appear in the *Kaliyuga*—even the great truths of Hinduism suffered deterioration in this age. According to Guru Nanak, even "the name of God becomes Allah in the *Kaliyuga*," reflecting the realities of this age, the declined status of Dharma, the diminished being of man and the impoverished state of his mind and heart.

The Voice of India is bringing out this reprint on the life of Muhammad by an eminent European Arabist in order to promote informed interest on the subject of Islam amongst Indian intellectuals. The best thing would have been if India had developed its own scholarship on this and other allied subjects; but seeing that it has not been able to do this so far, the next best thing is that it benefits from what others have done. Let us hope that from these beginnings will grow an indigenous scholarship with its own perspective and framework. Hitherto we have looked on Hinduism through the eyes of Islam and Christianity. Let us now learn to look at these ideologies from the vantage-point of Hindu spirituality—they are no more than ideologies, lacking as they are in the integrality and inwardness of true religion and spirituality. Such an exercise would also throw light on the self-destructiveness of the modern ideologies of Communism and Imperialism, inheritors of the prophetic mission or "burden", in its secularized version, of Christianity and Islam. The perspective gained will be a great corrective and will add a new liberating dimension; it will help not only India and Hinduism but the whole world.

A fateful thing has been happening. The East is waking up from its slumber. The wisdom of Hinduism, Buddhism, Taoism and Confucianism is becoming available to the world. Already, it is having a transforming effect on the minds of the people, particularly in countries where there is freedom to seek and express. Dogmas are under a cloud; claims on behalf of Last Prophethood and Only Sonship, hitherto enforced through great intellectual conditioning, browbeating, and the big stick, are becoming unacceptable. Religions of proxy are in retreat. More and more men now seek authentic experience. Borrowed creed will not do. Men and women are ceasing to be obedient believers and are becoming seekers. They no longer want to be anybody's sheep, now that they know that they can be their own shepherds. An external authority, even when it is called God in certain scriptures, threatening and promising alternately, is increasingly making less and less impression; people now realize that Godhead is their own true, secret status and they seek it in the depth of their own being. All this is in keeping with the wisdom of the East.

Two

HINDU VIEW OF CHRISTIANITY AND ISLAM*

(Muir on what *Lives of Muhammad* should be like—Muir's *Life* for thinking Muslims—Missionary angle—Similarities between Christianity and Islam—Christianity as Islam without Muhammad—Debate—"Idolatry" as common enemy—Monotheism—its origin—Pre-Islamic Arabs—Prophetism, an adjunct of Monotheism—Genesis of Religious Intolerance—Yogic spirituality—Advaita—Reincarnation—Christianity and Islam as Intruders—Europe, the Americas, the Middle East, Africa seeking their spiritual roots—How Hinduism can help them in their self-discovery).

Sir William Muir's *The Life of Mahomet* was first published in 1861 in four volumes, a pioneering study based wholly on orthodox original sources. An abridged edition came out in 1876. The third edition was published with important alterations in one volume in 1894. After Muir's *Life* many Lives of the Prophet have appeared, but it still remains a classic and in some ways has not yet been surpassed in comprehensiveness and in the wealth of material. Thanks to Archeology and other related disciplines, today we know a great deal more about pre-Islamic Arabian culture, but ever since Muir there has been no addition in the source material relating to the Prophet's life. This was exhausted long ago by early Muslim writers and all this was taken into account by Muir.

Muir belonged to the highest rung of British officialdom in India, but his reputation as an outstanding Arabist and Islamist has proved the most enduring. But he was also a believing Christian and his scholarly labours had a missionary motivation at heart. The motivation gave him a certain direction and a certain way of looking at things, but it did not compromise his

*Introduction to the reprint of *The Life of Mahomet* by Sir William Muir.

scholarship. In fact, he thought that for the very success of the Missionary enterprise, a good biography of the Prophet, based on unimpeachable sources respected by orthodox Muslim scholars, was a first necessary step. While discussing the inaccuracies of Washington Irving's *Life of Muhammad*, he stressed the need for a "life of the Prophet of Arabia which is based on sound, orthodox Muslim sources."

In his various articles which he wrote during mid-1840s and which appeared in the *Calcutta Review*, we easily get to know what he expected his *Life* to be and to achieve. He wanted it to oppose two kinds of Lives that were current: one was by Missionary writers who were careless about their facts, slipshod in their scholarship, hostile in intent, unsympathetic in treatment, and uninhibited in expressing their opinions. For example, A. Sprenger, his contemporary, a Missionary and an Islamist of great repute, regarded Muhammad as having a "weak and cunning mind." Muir disagreed and argued that such a man "could never have accomplished the mighty mission which Mahomet wrought." Others called Islam "a spurious faith," and its founder "a false prophet" and a "counterfeit Messiah." Muir probably shared these opinions, but he discouraged their too open expression. He thought that if the Missionaries used such epithets, how could they get the hearing of the Muslims? He probably also thought that stating facts should do, for they would speak for themselves.

He also wanted his *Life* to oppose Biographies of the Prophet written by native Muslim writers which were current among devout Muslims. These were highly fanciful and extravagant and were based on fabricated traditions of which the early biographers of the Prophet were quite innocent. For illustration, Muir discussed a biography of the Prophet, *Moulud Sharīf* or "The Ennobled Nativity" written by Ghulam Imam Shahid, an Indian Muslim, during the 1840s. It was very popular among the Muslims and it had already seen a dozen editions. In this biography, the author, an ornate writer, informed us how Allah wishing to manifest himself formed the "light of Muhammad a thousand years before creation"; how when the light was at last transferred to the womb of Ameena, Muhammad's mother, "200 damsels of the Coreish died of envy"; how angels rejoiced at his birth; how, as he came out of the womb he was already circumcised; and how he repeated the kalima.

Muir tells us that early traditions relating to the Prophet's nativity contain no such material. He wanted his *Life* to be faithful to this early tradition, and he thought that such a biography would be respected by the Muslims and would therefore serve the Missionary cause better. He argued: "If we can from their own best sources, prove to them that they are deceived and superstitious in many important points... we shall have gone a great way to excite honest inquiry and induce the sincere investigator to follow our lead." He wanted to present this biography to "thinking Mohammedans, who are turning their attention to the historical evidence of their faith; and are comparing them with those of Christianity." In this way, he thought, rather fondly, that "thinking Muslims" would come to prefer Christianity to their own faith. How the stories of the Immaculate Conception, the Virgin Mother, the Only Begotten Son will satisfy their historical sense is not made clear. In fact, some of the "thinking Mohammedans" on whom Muir so much relied remained unmoved by Muir's labour of love. Sayyid Ahmad (later Sir Sayyid), who wrote his own Biography of the Prophet in reply to Muir's, argued whether the biblical miracles of Moses and Jesus should not be considered from the same rational viewpoint. But in their turn, the Christians were dogmatic and they had learnt to believe that while the miracles of Jesus were historical and well attested, those found in rival faiths were irrational.

II

As Missionary scholars studied Islam, mostly with a view to convert Muslims, they found that there was a lot in common between it and their own faith. Both were Judaic in origin and orientation, and both had common prophets. The biblical prophets including Jesus are highly honoured in the Quran. Both shared a common God and a common line of prophets, and both believed in Revelation from the same God. In fact, the prophet of Islam claimed that he communicated with the same God who communicated with Moses and Jesus, and that he was merely reviving the old religion of Ibrahim, the common patriarch of them all. In this revival, he expected the Jews and the Christians to play their part and enlist under his banner. He felt that he was sent to the "people of the Book" as much as to the Arabs. "O ye people of the Book! our Apostle has come to you to explain to you much of what you have hidden of the Book," Allah told them (Quran 5.18). But by and large, they disappointed him. However, the Prophet still kept his hope, particularly in the Christians. On one occasion, Allah assured him that though the Jews and the idolaters are "the strongest in enmity" towards him, but those who call themselves Christians, "you will find the nearest in love...[and] when they hear what has been revealed to the Prophet, you will see their eyes gush with tears at what they recognize as truth therein" (Quran 5.85, 86).

The Missionaries in turn felt a similar affinity towards Islam and expected much from it. With so much in common — "a one and living God; Mosaic traditions; nay, a belief in Christ," as Sir Robert B. Edwardes, Commissioner and Governor-General's Agent at Peshawar put it—the Muslims should find no difficulty in converting to Christianity. In fact, according to him they should do very well as converts, and in support he quoted his Bible: "For if thou were cut out of the live tree which is wild by nature, and were grafted contrary to nature into a good live tree: how much more shall these, which be the natural branches, be grafted into their own live tree" (Rom.11.24).

But not all shared this bright vision and Muir was one of them. He agreed that Christians had many advantages in the contest. "We have no infidel view to oppose; the existence of sin, and its future punishment is allowed; the necessity of revelation, and even the Divine origin of the Old and New Testament dispensation, are conceded; the most of the attributes of God, the immaculate conception of Christ, the miracles which attested His mission, are all admitted," Muir said. But he still felt that this convergence was of no avail. For, the Muslims believed in

Jesus not because of the Bible but because of the Quran, and his study of the Quran had convinced him that the "object of Mahomet was entirely to supersede Christianity", and that the conditions upon which he "permitted Christianity to exist were those of sufferance."

He argued that since the Quran has taken much from the Bible, it therefore abounds with approaches to truth. And this very fact fortifies the Muslims in their present position. "It is a melancholy truth," Muir said, that "a certain amount of light and knowledge often renders only the more difficult to drive the bigot from his prejudices." As a result, the supposed advantages, the points common to both, "are thus turned into a barrier against us, into a thick impenetrable veil which effectually excludes every glimmer of the true light," Muir added.

III

Some Missionaries wondered why Islam should have in the first instance succeeded at all considering that Christianity was already there in the field and the good news was already known. They believed that the founder of Islam came into contact with a corrupt form of Christianity and that had he known the purer type, the story would have been very different. Isaac Taylor says in his *Ancient Christianity*, Vol I, that the Christianity which Muhammad and his Khalifahs knew "was a superstition so abject, an idolatry so gross and shameless, church doctrines so arrogant, church practices so dissolute and so puerile, that the strong-minded Arabians felt themselves inspired anew as God's messengers to reprove the errors of the world, and authorized as God's avengers to punish apostate Christendom." Muir expresses the same thought and regrets that a purer Christianity like the one represented by the Anglican Church was not there at hand when Muhammad appeared on the scene.

Sir Monier Williams, a Sanskritist with deep Missionary concerns, speculated in the same vein: "If only the self-deluded but fervent-spirited Muhammad, whose soul was stirred within him when he saw his fellow town-men wholly given to idolatry, had been brought into association with the purer form of Christianity... he might have died a martyr for the truth, Asia might have numbered her millions of Christians, and the name of Saint Muhammad might have been in the calendar of our Book of Common Prayer... Think, then, of the difference in the present condition of the Asiatic world, if the fire of Muhammad's eloquence had been kindled, and the force of his personal influence exerted on the side of veritable Christianity" (*Modern India*, 1878).

A new opportunity came again for Christianity when Europe, and particularly England, dominated the world during the last few centuries. During this while, one would have expected, according to Muir, that Christian Europe would have improved its advantages for evangelizing the East, that "Britain, the bulwark of religion in the West, would have stepped forth as its champion in the East, and displayed her faith and her zeal where they were most urgently required." But, alas! it was not to be so and, Muir continues, "England was then sadly neglectful of her responsibility; her religion was shown only at home and she was careless of the spiritual darkness of her benighted subjects abroad; her sons, who adopted India as their country, so far from endeavouring to impart to its inhabitants the benefits of their religion, too often banished it from their own minds, and exhibited to heathens [Hindus] and Mohammadans the sad spectacle of men without faith...[and] their lives too often presented a practical and powerful, a constant and a living, argument against the truth of our holy faith."

IV

Though so much alike and having the same origin, Christianity and Islam quarrelled. They quarrelled as soon as they came face to face. For centuries they fought with fire and sword. At one time, it seemed that Islam had won and it was knocking at the door of Europe. But after much labour and luck, the tide was turned. In the long interval of armed peace that followed, Europe greatly improved its weaponry and its military position could not be challenged. Meanwhile, it also added another weapon to its arsenal—ideological warfare.

Islam had no way of meeting this challenge. It could not deal with Christians in the old way, the only way it knew, the way of the sword. It had to listen to the "arguments" of the Christian West with respect and even allow some sort of freedom and physical security to the Christians and the Jews in the countries it dominated.

Meanwhile, many things had taken place in Europe. It had passed through a period of rationalism and it began to discuss Christianity with a new freedom. As a result, it was now less Christian, and it did not apply the Spanish solution to the Muslim problem.

But it did recognize the usefulness of Christianity for the empire, and the Missionaries had a fairly free field. They were still discouraged from a too blatant use of force, but they were well-endowed and they had great political prestige; they often worked in collusion with the white administrators. They fully utilized these advantages.

They had also developed what they call *Apologetics*, the art of establishing the truths of Christianity and controverting those of other faiths.

The Muslims were new to the art of religious discussion—their *forte* had been of a different kind—and initially they were at a disadvantage. But they picked up the art soon, and did quite well. The Missionaries tried to prove Jesus with the help of the Quran, Muslims tried to prove Muhammad's mission with the help of the Bible. The former argued that Christianity was Islam without Muhammad—no great matter according to them; that Muhammad himself had recognized Jesus as an Apostle and Muslims should have no difficulty in going a bit further and recognize him as the only Son and the Saviour. The latter argued that Muhammad's mission was prophesied in the Bible itself and in recognizing him as the last spokesman of God, Christians would only be true to their own scriptures.

Thus they bluffed each other and the game continued for some time. But they could not always keep the mask on. The Missionaries often let out that Islam was only an inferior reproduction of Christianity, an imitation of the original but not the original itself, and that Muhammad was obviously a pretender; Muslims argued that Muhammad's revelation was the last one and the Judaic and Christian revelations already stood abrogated. There is in fact a belief among the Muslims based on a *hadīs* that Jesus in his Second Coming will be born a faithful Muslim, will fight for Islam, "judge Christians, break crosses, kill swine, and abolish *jizia*" (*Sahih Muslim*, 287)—*jizia* would be rendered superfluous as all Christians would become Muslims.

The controversy was sharp, as it often is between creeds which are alike in beliefs and aims and methods—like Stalinists and Trotskyites. Both claimed to believe in the same God, but each claimed sole heirship to his throne. Muir found in Islam "a subtle usurper, who climbed into the throne under pretence of legitimate succession, and seized upon the forces of the crown to supplant its authority." He also found in it a "dangerous adversary" who "has borrowed so many weapons of Christianity." Muslims argued that had the Jews and the Christians not falsified their scriptures, they would have long back joined the banner of Islam.

The debate had some interesting features. Each side was *rational* about the faith of the other, but not about its own. As a result, though Muslims fully utilized the rational critique to which Christianity was subjected by Europe during its recent Age of Reason, they had no use for it for themselves. Hence Muslims yet know no real self-criticism except to say that they are not Muslim enough!

Another feature was that even though the language of the debate was often sharp, its parameters were limited; they consisted of a single God who communicates with his followers through a privileged single medium, and who exercises an unbending enmity towards heathens and infidels. Throughout the debate, these premises remained unquestioned and no awareness was shown of the concerns of a deeper spirituality.

Though Christianity and Islam quarrelled between themselves, their real and ultimate target remained "Idolatry"— their name for all non-Semitic religions, which means all religions of the past and most religions of the present. The Missionary writers highly appreciated Islam's role in "cleansing the world from the scourge of idolatry, and for preparing the way for the reception of a purer faith." Similarly, Islam recognized Christians as "people of the Book," no small honour and no small point of security. This recognition allowed the Christians to practise their faith under certain disabilities and also provided some sort of physical security to their persons, something which was denied by Muslim Arab rulers to their own blood brothers, who had to submit to a choice between Islam and death.

V

It is well-known that Christians and Muslims derived their much-vaunted Monotheism from the Jews, but the Jews themselves were not monotheists in the beginning. Like other neighbouring peoples, they had their tribal god towards whom they felt a special loyalty but it did not occur to them yet to deny the gods of others. True, the gods sometimes quarrelled as their followers quarrelled, yet it was still far from the thought of the Jews to deny "other" gods. That other gods did not exist or were false, and that their god alone was true and enjoyed some sort of universal sovereignty, was a later development. This development had to wait till the arrival of their Prophets, beginning with Moses.

It seems that the early Jews did not know Jehovah according to the biblical testimony itself. "By name Jehovah was I not known to them," says the Bible (Exod. 6.3). Probably, the Jews borrowed Egyptian Gods, at least in some measure, while they were in Egypt and they continued worshipping them even during the days of their wanderings in the desert. There are also indications that the new religion, whatever it was and whenever adopted, was imposed against great opposition and with great ferocity. While Jehovah revealed himself to Moses as the only God of the Jews, they were worshipping another God under the symbol of a Bull (Has it something to do with *Nandī* of Hinduism?), a mode they had probably adopted in Egypt. "Slay every man his brother, and every man his companion, and every man his neighbour," ordered Jehovah to those who truly followed him. Three thousand men were killed in a day and a new religion was inaugurated or an old one established.[1] The killers were consecrated and they became the priestly class, the Levites.

Some thinkers believe that Moses had borrowed the idea of a single God while in Egypt under the influence of Akhnaton's religious reforms. But this God was too mild and pacific, and would not do for the new life of the Jews. Therefore, during their wanderings, they adopted another God, the God of Midianites, a Volcano God. And that is how they acquired a god who was both militant as well as single. He became the God of the Jews and they became His people. Freud says that a God of this nature was "better suited to a people who were starting out to occupy a new homeland by force." He promised them "a land flowing with milk and honey," while he urged them to exterminate its inhabitants "with the edge of the sword" (Exod. 3.8; Deut.13.15).

As events settled, many Jewish scholars tried to allegorize the events of Exodus and ethicalize their God. The Talmuds, as these commentaries are called, contain much that is noble and inspiring. But the biblical tradition still remained strong. Its God could not shed his jealousy and his exclusive character, and it continued to regard the Gods of other people as "abominations."

In course of time, this God in all his exclusiveness and jealousy was adopted by Christianity and Islam. In fact, in their hands, he became still more exclusive and jealous. He also became more ambitious and bellicose. While with the Jews, he remained their God alone; but, except spasmodically, he refused to be the God of others. Other people had to make do with their own Gods, howsoever "false," and these Gods had to be content with their own followers, howsoever benighted and out of grace with Jehovah. But things changed with the advent of Christianity

[1]But Jehovah continued to be worshipped under the form of a Bull or Golden Calf for quite many centuries. There are repeated reference to this fact in the Old Testament (Num. 23.22; 24.8; Hosea 8.5, 6; 13.2; 1Kings 12.28-30). Jehovah also continued to be worshipped as a brazen serpent till Hezekiah destroyed it (2 Kings 18.4).

and Islam. Through them, Jehovah came into his own and He offered to be the God of all. He asked his followers to go in all directions and preach His name, to "go out into the highways and hedges, and compel people to come in." He armed them and asked them to declare from the housetops several times a day that He alone was true and that other Gods were false. Others could refuse this invitation or call at their own peril, spiritual and physical. As His followers became more powerful, the peril became increasingly more physical.

There was another difference. Though the Jewish God was single, yet he spoke through many mouths. Moses was probably the most important, but a plurality of prophethood was recognized. It is unfortunate that the Judaic religion could not take full advantage of this principle. As the Mosaic-Monotheistic tradition was too strong, in practice the Prophetic message tended to be the same—more of the same Mosaic God. For the same reason, even movements like those represented by the Essenes, influenced by Hinduism-Buddhism, could not break away sufficiently from that tradition. But the principle of plurality of prophethood is in itself important, and some day it may become a source of significant spiritual changes.

Pre-Islamic Arabs

Monotheism of the Semitic kind was also unknown to Pre-Islamic Arabs.[2] They very well knew the Jews and the Christians but they had no particular attraction for their God. They had their own Gods and they were perfectly satisfied with them. The more religious of the Arabs who sought a deeper contact with their Gods often retired to the hills in their vicinity and engaged themselves in fasts and vigils. Muhammad also did it and in this he was following a long-established practice of his people.

But they were surrounded by neighbours who followed a faith which had a single God and a single Prophet. Traders

[2]Among the Arabs and the Phoenicians, *el, eloah, elohim, lāh,* were common names for a God. But following the political fortunes of his votaries, a *lāh, a* god, also became *al-lāh, the* God, and underwent enlargement without showing any corresponding moral improvement.

returning from these lands brought news of how powerful and rich they were and how they were connected with the most powerful Empire of the time. Thus monotheism and prophetism were already prestigious creeds and they could not be without attraction for some persons.

Muhammad was one of those persons who were attracted by the new creed. He adopted the God of his powerful neighbours and claimed that He communicated with him as He had earlier communicated with Abraham, Moses and Jesus; that in fact his communication updated earlier communications and even abrogated them. He told his people that they had been worshipping false Gods, and that they should now take to the true one of his preaching. In his preaching, he also insisted that he was not only the latest but also the last apostle of this true God.

There was a long struggle. The Prophet harangued, castigated, mocked, denounced, fulminated against the traditional Gods of his people but without being able to move them. In the process, at one stage, he even felt isolated. In this state of mind, he recognized the traditional deities as worthy intermediaries. The Meccans were pleased and offered to make up. But the Prophet began to have doubts and thought that the conciliatory verses were inspired by Satan. These are called Satanic verses which, thanks to Salman Rushdie episode, are widely talked about but without many knowing what these are about. But from a deeper spiritual angle, these were probably the most Angelic of the Quranic verses.

The Prophet took up haranguing and ridiculing again. He appealed to the Arabs' patriotic feeling that his was an Arabic revelation, something which God had hitherto neglected to send, and that he was sent to the Arabs as their prophet, the only prophet ever sent to them. But the people argued that he was a poet, or a soothsayer, or was plainly out of his mind. He insisted that he was a prophet. It is not certain what the Meccans objected to, whether to the idea of a a single God or to Muhammad being His prophet, but the tussle continued, and he held out threats against their disbelief. He told them what they were heading for. Verily the day was not far off when they would cry in vain: "Yea! a warner came to us, and we called him liar...Had we but listened or had sense we had not been amongst the fellows of the Blaze"— the Quranic name for Hell.

As the Prophet gained strength, he supplemented spiritual threats with physical ones, while the Arabs observed constraints of their tribal code. The Meccans were waylaid, their caravans looted and eventually Mecca itself was invaded. The traditional idols were pulled down and their shrines were converted into houses of the new God. The Arabs were given an option between conversion and death. The story of Arab resistance to the new religion and how it broke down under superior force is ably shown by Sita Ram Goel in his *Hindu Temples: What Happened to Them,* Part II. Those interested in the subject may find it there.

But force alone would not have sufficed. The new creed was also found attractive economically and politically. The believers were promised not only houris in paradise but they were also given a share in the booty accruing from new religious wars that were becoming the order of the day; they also had a share in the large revenues coming from a fast expanding Muslim Empire. Every Arab was drafted as a soldier of Islam and his name was put on payroll. Umar regularized the system. Every Arab was a partner in the revenues derived from the loot and exploitation of the newly conquered lands — Muslim brotherhood in action. The scales were fixed according to one's nearness to the Prophet. The widows of Muhammad received an annual allowance of 10,000 dirhams each; the famous Three Hundred of the Battle of Badr had 5,000 dirhams each; those of the Pledge of the Tree received 4,000 each; every one who had converted to Islam before the Battle of Badr got 4,000 each, and their children 2,000 dirhams each; and so on, they graduated downwards to 200 dirhams. Wives, widows, and children had each their share. Every Muslim had a share in this classification. Officers of the Arab Occupation Armies in different cantonment areas of the Empire received yearly from 6,000 to 9,000 dirhams; and every boy, as soon as born, received 100 dirhams each; every Muslim had the title to be entered on the payroll, with a minimum annual allowance of ten pieces, rising with advancing age to its proper place. For a fuller account of the Civil List (*Diwan*), one can refer to the *Tārikh-i-Tabarī* (Khilāfat Rāshida, Part I, Urdu, Nafis Academy, Karachi).

These stipends were hereditary, and they created a class of people who lived on the fat of the land they occupied. They laid the foundation of a thorough imperialism which was more durable than any other the world had known in the past. And this is how a people who had been hitherto upright and chivalrous, became a great scourge and cruel invaders and rulers. Their ethical code suffered a great decline.[3] They began to live on the labour and sweat of others.

But the greatest decline was in the concept of their Godhead which was at the root of all other kinds of degradation. Their new God was "one"; it was male; it was exclusive and intolerant; it took pride in refusing "partnership" with "other" Gods—whatever that may mean. It was also different from their accustomed Gods in another important sense: their traditional Gods spoke to them directly, but the new one dealt with them through an intermediary.

Pagan Arabs were a tolerant people. In fact, many Christians and Jews had found shelter with them; they were fleeing away from the intolerance of their own fellow religious men in the neighbouring countries. But as soon as the Pagan Arabs became Muslim, it was a different thing. Jews and Christians were turned out of the land of Arabia. Pagan Arabia accepted Jews and Christians but rejected their God for itself; Muslim Arabia embraced their God but rejected His people. This is a measure of the difference between the two approaches: Pagan and Se-

[3]Margoliouth shows how and when it happened, how "men who had never broken an oath learnt that they might evade their obligations... men to whom the blood of the kinsmen had been as their own began to shed it with impunity in the cause of God; ... [how] lying and treachery in the cause of Islam received divine approval, hesitation to perjure oneself in that cause being represented as a weakness... [how] Moslems became distinguished by the obscenity of their language... [how] coveting of goods and wives (possessed by Unbelievers) was avowed without discouragement from the Prophet" (*Mohammed and the Rise of Islam*, p. 149).

mitic. Paganism has multiple Gods but believes in one humanity; Semitic religions have one God but at least two humanities: believers on one hand and unbelievers or infidels or heathens on the other. The division is not just social, or racial, or cultural; it is *metaphysical.* Believers owe nothing to infidels, not even ordinary ethical behaviour. The Quran requires that Muslims "are vehement against misbelievers, but kind amongst themselves" (48.29).

VI

Prophetism

The theory of a single God had a necessary adjunct in the theory of a single Prophet or Saviour or Interpreter. The two theories have a family likeness and go together. In fact, as the Semitic God was becoming one, he was also becoming exclusive in his communication. Even when he had a chosen people, these people had no direct approach to Him. He told them that He will send them a prophet and "will tell him what to say and he will tell the people everything I command. He will speak in my name and I shall punish anyone who refuses to obey him."

In due course, the intermediary became more than a medium. In Christianity, he became the Saviour; in Islam, he became the Intercessor and also the last Prophet through whom God ever spoke.

Claims began to be made on his behalf, claims almost as tall as for the God he represented. In fact, the God tended to become redundant and the intermediary took his place, who in turn was re-presented by his own nominees. The New Testament says: "Salvation is to be found through him (Jesus) alone; in all the world there is no one else whom God has given who can save us" (Acts 4.12). At another place it says: "God put all things under Christ's feet and gave him to the Church as the supreme Lord over all things." Such claims are offensive to man's rational as well as to his spiritual sense, but they have proved highly profitable to those who speak in the name of these intermediaries. Now they represent a great vested interest.

Intolerance

Intolerance must be the fruit of such bitter seeds. Other Gods must be dethroned, and so must also die those who speak in the name of other Gods (Deut.18.18-19).

The Semitic God is jealous, and so is his sole prophet. Just like his God, he too can brook no rivals. Jesus tells us that "all who came before me are thieves and robbers" (Jn.10.8). He warns his flock again and again against rival claimants. "Beware of false prophets who come to you in sheep's clothing, but inwardly are ravenous wolves"(Mt.7.15; or 24.4). Muhammad admitted some prophets in the past in order to give his own prophethood an ancestry, but he abolished further prophethood. He was the latest and also the last prophet, the seal of Prophecy.

The fact is that intolerance is inbuilt into the basic Semitic approach and cursing comes naturally to it. The Bible is full of curses invoked on rivals — gods, prophets, apostles, doctrines. For example, Paul told his Galatian followers that "should anyone preach to you a gospel contrary to that which we preached to you, let him be accursed." This tradition has continued and has been the strongest element in Christianity, whether Catholic or non-Catholic. For example, the "Articles of Religion" of the Anglican Church lays down: "They also are to be had accursed that presume to say, That every man shall be saved by the Law or Sect which he professeth... For holy Scripture set out unto us only the Name of Jesus Christ, whereby men must be saved."

Christians claim that Jesus is an incarnation. One is not sure what he incarnated, but it is not difficult to see that Christianity incarnated a new religious intolerance, a tradition which Islam also faithfully continued. Religious intolerance was there before, but it was spasmodic and it was not supported by a theology. It was with the coming of Christianity and Islam that religious bigotry and arrogance descended on the earth on a large scale and with a new power. They know so little about themselves but they claim to know everything about God, and in imposing their definition upon others, they have killed millions of people. They have been even more fanatic about their founders. "If you won't believe that you're redeemed by *my* redeemer's blood, I'll drown you in your own," says the Christian, to put it in the language of Aldous Huxley. The same is true of Muslims. In their practice, Muhammad has been more central to their religion than their One God. You could jest about this God but woe unto him who jests about the Prophet. His punishment is death: *Bā khudā dīwānā bāsh, wa bā muhammad hoshiyār.*

Some apologists of Islam say that Islam was better in the beginning and that intolerance is a latter-day growth. But it is not so. According to Margoliouth, "Islam was intolerant in the beginning as it is to-day." Intolerance is part of its very creed. It is a declaration of war, a battle-cry against non-Muslims and their Gods, and historically it began so and continues to be so. Five times a day, a pious Muslim is expected to declare that the Gods of others are false and that only *his* God is true.

If religious tolerance is a value, Christianity as well as Islam lack it badly. Wherever they have gone, they have carried fire and sword and oppressed and destroyed so far as it lay in their power. They demolished and occupied the temples and shrines of others. Any tolerance shown was an exception, intolerance was the rule. Hindus know to some extent what the Muslims did, but the Christian record in this matter has not been less thorough. For that one has to know the history of Christianity in Europe,[4] North Africa, Americas, and even in South India under the Portuguese and the French. As Ishwar Sharan observes in his *The Myth of Saint Thomas and the Mylapore Shiva Temple*, "Aurangzeb is nobody in comparison to St. Xavier when it comes to temple-breaking and bloodshed." Their record has been matched only recently by Communism, considered a Christian heresy by thinkers like Bertrand Russell. In China, the communist regime destroyed half a million Buddhist shrines. (Were

[4]Christian history in Europe is full of great vandalism in which Christian "saints" played a most conspicuous role. St. Maurillius burnt idols in Gaul; St. Firminus of Amiens destroyed them wherever he found them; St. Columban and St. Gall destroyed shrines, groves and images on the Continent, especially in Germany, and St. Augustine in England. Another Saint, Gregory, also a monk, destroyed, among many pagan temples, two Vaishnava temples in Syria, built by Hindu colonists there, in 304 A.D., even before Christianity was adopted by the Roman Emperor.

the Buddhists there also in the habit of hoarding their gold in their shrines, thus attracting communist expropriatory justice and getting them destroyed in the process? Or was it a rare example of an act purely motivated by an ideology? Probably Stalinist historians of the JNU would like to explain.)

VII

It is obvious that this ideology of a single god, a single prophet, a single revelation, a single church or *ummah,* and also of a single life and single judgement (Hebr. 9.27) is very different from the one the world at large has known in the past or even at the present. Historically speaking, it is more of an aberration, a local vogue which consolidated itself through conquest and propaganda, and it could impose itself in no other way. It is different not only from polytheism, a religious expression at a more popular level, but also from mystical religions expressing man's more intensive search for a spiritual life. It is certainly different from the spirituality known in the East by Hermetics, Stoics, Pythagoreans, Taoists and Vedantists; it is different from them in most matters, particularly in its concept of deity, man, and nature; it is different in its definitions, modes, theory and praxis.

Man is a born worshipper and has an innate need for God. Therefore, all peoples and cultures have a God in one form or another. But the word does not mean the same thing everywhere, even within a single culture; it represents different grades and levels. Ordinarily, the concept of God is much mixed up with man's lower needs and nature and God is sometimes no more than a glorified Pharaoh or Caligula. But such a God cannot last long unless this meaning is frozen and made enduring with the help of a theology. More often, a God has to have other, more humane qualities and serve more humane ends. He has to be a helper and a guide and provide solace and succor to man in his difficulties — and sometimes even in his more questionable designs, like his designs against his enemies who may have done no wrong to him.

This much of God is enough for most people, but it will not

do for all. Some seek a deeper meaning, a more final explanation of life, a higher law of conduct; they seek to find out Who they are, Where they come from, Where they are going. In short, they raise questions about their origins, their self-identity, their true home. They seek a transformed life; they seek to be led from the unreal to the real, from darkness to light, from death to immortality.

All higher spirituality in general and Hindu spirituality in particular has concerned itself with these questions. It has found that questions about Gods are ultimately questions about one's own true Self. It has also found that man lives for the most part in his external self, in his desires, hates, ego and nescience, and that this veils his true soul-life. It has found that in order to uncover this higher life, man has to purify his instruments of knowing, and develop new powers of the soul, like faith, *tapas*, self-restraint, harmlessness, truthfulness, steadfastness, forgiveness; he has to develop powers of concentration and meditation; he has to develop devotion, spiritual discrimination, detachment, equal-mindedness and universality.

As he goes within, he enters into new realms and realities hitherto unknown. He meets many psychic formations and spiritual beings of various grades of purity and power corresponding to his own purity, needs and readiness. He also meets desire-gods and ego-gods and if sufficient purity is not established in the soul, he may identify himself with one of them; he may then declare that *his god* is *the God*, and he may prophetically demand that his God be worshipped by all.

On this journey, the pilgrim sees God or Gods as powers of the soul, and he also finds that the qualities that satisfy and nourish the soul the most are also the most God-like—the *daivī sampad* of thc Gita. Here the deity does not take particular pride in being single or object to being multiple, for it knows that it is both. Here there is no "jealous" God at war with "other" Gods; here Gods are friends, and each images all. Here the soul also discovers that it is kin to the deity, and like unto that which it worships.

Here a man may come to know that he is one with the

Father, but that is not enough. He must also know that this is true of all. But Christian Theology says that while Jesus was one with God, the rest are one with Adam. The exclusive Sonship is a gratuitous and non-spiritual assumption.

Here one also does not find the "one" God of Semitic persuasion, but one discovers a new togetherness of all things, a unity holding all. The soul sees itself in all. Here a man is one with all humanity; in fact, with all living beings and even with all elements. Here one feels friendliness towards all. There are no infidels and heathens here.

Yoga

It is not all just a "funny feeling," as an American Jesuit friend described it. It is a deeper spirituality, a deeper conception of God that develops when one knows how to dive deep into oneself. It is science and art of inward journey developed by the Hindus and called by them *Yoga*. We cannot discuss the subject adequately here, but we have already mentioned some of its features above and that should suffice for our purpose here. Yoga is a special contribution made by religions belonging to the *Sanātana Dharma* family.

Hindu spirituality seeks Self-Knowledge, or *ātma-jñāna*. This also leads to the highest knowledge of Gods. In fact, without *ātma-vāda*, there cannot be developed *deva-vāda*. Here the deity is known in deep meditation by a mind at its most luminous and intuitive, *dhyāna-gamya* and *buddhi-gamya*; he is seated in the cave of the heart (*guhāhitam*, and *hridayastha*), or he resides inside the lotus-plexus situated between the two eyes (*ājñāchakrābja-nilaya*), or in the thousand-petalled *chakra* in the crown of the head (*sahasradalapadmastha*). All these are Yogic concepts based on a deep knowledge of man's inner topography, his spiritual body in touch with larger subtle worlds and spiritual cosmic forces and powers. There is nothing analogous to them in most other religions. Jehovah and Allah are non-Yogic Gods,[5] belonging to non-Yogic religions—religions

[5]It is not that Semitic religions had no better model. They must have known the surrounding Hermetic, Pythagorean, even Vedantic and Bud-

which are more like ideologies than spiritualities. They are self-regarding Gods and embody an intolerant idea. They do not project a too happy psyche, and as their source is not a *dhyāna-bhūmi* sufficiently deep and pure, they would hardly do for the Gods of developed spiritualities. Readers who are interested in this approach to the problem may refer to our Introduction to *Inner Yoga* by Sri Anirvan.

The "oneness" attributed to these non-yogic Gods is different from the "oneness" of a yogic God. The oneness of the latter is like the oneness of the sky which pervades all, which is everywhere and is in all; it contains everything, though it is contained by none; it is *advaita*, undifferentiated reality, not the monadity of numbered things. A yogic God is a *unity*, not a *unit*; it is compatible with "other" Gods, includes them, and is mani-

---

dhist traditions but they fought off these influences. For example, early Christianity had a Gnostic tradition which opposed Jehovah, the biblical God — male, one, and jealous. The *Secret Book of John*, a Gnostic work, says that when Jehovah "in his madness", declared that "I am God, and there is no other beside me", he was "ignorant of... the place from which he came", and that in declaring that he was a jealous God and there was no other God, he proves " that another God does exist; for if there was no other one, of whom would he be jealous?" Similarly, another Gnostic work said that when Jehovah boasted that there was no other God, "he sinned against all the immortal ones."

The story of Islam is no different. Prophetic Islam is inimical to mystic ideas. In the beginning, some Sufis courted martyrdom, but eventually they bought peace and safety by surrendering to Prophetic Islam. There have been some outstanding Sufis, but by and large the Sufi movement has been part of a larger aggressive apparatus, just like Christian Missions of Imperialism. Though Islam persecuted "infidels", destroyed their temples, enslaved and looted them, we find no Sufis protesting. In fact, they were often beneficiaries of this vandalism. "In many cases there is no doubt that the shrine of a Muslim saint marks the site of some local cult which was practised on the spot long before the introduction of Islam," says Thomas Arnold making it look quite normal and harmless. Mu'īn al-Dīn Chishtī's dargaḥ at Ajmer is one such shrine built on the ruins of an old Hindu temple. The saint had also got the present of a Hindu princess, part of the booty captured by a Muslim General, Malik Khitab, when he attacked the neighbouring pagan land. Sufi saints often took full part in Islamic *jihād*. R.M. Eaton's *Sufis of Bijapur*, published by Princetone University (1978), illustrates it amply. No wonder, the book has been banned by the Government of India.

fested by them. The *advaitic*-God of the Yogas and the Puranas is not the *monad*-God of the Bible and the Quran.

Reincarnation

A spirituality based on Yoga also makes a man aware of the great law of *karma* of inscrutable working; through it he becomes aware of the forces of inertia and the forces of transformation; he becomes aware of many lives he has lived and the many lives he has yet to live. This is called the doctrine of Incarnation, Rebirth. But behind these repeated births, this spirituality also makes one aware of a state of the soul which is free and untainted, pure and immortal.

According to the doctrine of Reincarnation, it is the soul which carries the body and not the body which carries the soul. According to this belief, the soul exists before it takes on a body and after it quits it. This belief is universal and is widely shared. It is found among people who are called "primitive" as well as those who are called "civilized." It is found among the Eskimos, Australians, Melanesians, the Poso Alfur of Celebes in Indonesia, among Algonquians, Bantus, Finns and Lapps, old Teutonics and Druids, the Lithuanians and Lettish people, among the old Greeks and Romans and the Chinese. Plato believed that the soul is immortal and it participates in many incarnations. The doctrine was preached by Pythagoreans, and the teachers of Orphic mystery; it was named by them *metensomatosis*, or "changing of bodies", almost in the language of the Gita. It was also preached by Manicheans who once formed the most formidable opposition to Christianity. It holds a central place in Taoism and in all great religious systems forming part of *Sanātana Dharma*.

In short, the doctrine has the support of the spiritual intuition of most mankind, ancient or modern. It is strange that Semitic religions could do without it. There was a time when the belief was held by Christianity too, but it was given up at an early stage, strangely enough, first at the wishes of Empress Theodora. It was condemned at the Council of Constantinople (AD 543) as an Origenist error. "If anyone says or thinks that human souls had a previous existence—*anathema sit*," the

Council declared.

It had to do it. Following Plato, Basilides, Origen and many other early Christian writers believed that souls in their original purity pre-existed, that any punishment of hell was temporary, to be followed by the general restoration of all souls to their former state (*apokatastasis*). But this belief went completely against some of the most fundamental doctrines of Christianity: the doctrines of one life and one judgement, of pre-election, of some saved but many condemned to suffer eternal punishment in hell. Therefore, reincarnation had to be given up.

The idea could not have a better fate in Islam. The idea is known here as *tanāsukh* and we meet it only amongst the Druzes, and some heretic sects such as Ali Ilahis, who ask men not to fear death because death is like the dive the duck makes. But the idea is incompatible with mainstream Islam and, indeed, with all religious ideologies that lack spiritual spaces and believe in one life, and one judgement.

There are many other differences between Semitic religions and the spiritualities based on Yoga. The latter are little concerned, as one can easily find, with Vicarious Atonement, Begotten Sons, Last Prophets, Special Covenants, Chosen Churches or Ummas, proxies and surrogates, Missions and *jihād*, threats of hell and promises of a paradise, which are the staples of the former.

There is no wonder that Yoga is unwelcome to prophetic religions. It is subversive of dogmas and special claims, and is too universal in spirit. Only recently, in 1989, the Vatican issued a 23-page document, approved by Pope John Paul, to its monasteries and convents warning them against the lure of "Eastern meditation practices" which obscured "the Christian conception of prayer, its logic and requirements."

VIII

A New Thinking

Over most of the world, there is a new thinking on religious questions. In many countries, there is also a growing awareness that their present religions were imposed on them and that they themselves belonged to a different religious tradition. Ralph Borsodi, an American educationist and social thinker, in his *The Challenge of Asia* observes that "everywhere in the world excepting in Asia Minor, the three great Semitic religions—Judaism, Christianity and Islam—are intruders;" that "indigenous Asia is Brahmanist, Confucianist, Buddhist, Taoist; indigenous Europe is pagan;" that "in Europe, Christianity is a superimposition;[6] in Asia, Islam is."

As in many other things, Europe also leads this stir. It is witnessing a revival of its ancient religion; it is remembering its past and it is trying to throw off the yoke of Christianity and revive its old religious tradition that expressed itself in the language of Gods. Last year, the Pagans of Great Britain held a meeting attended by 300 representatives. They had met a year before, but their meeting was not allowed to be held by the Fundamental Christian Coalition. This time however they were able to hold their deliberations undisturbed. As reported in *Hinduism Today* (February, 1991), they said at the meeting that Christianity has buried them with a theology that has masculanized God, separated man from Divinity, and robbed the land of its sacredness. They promised to return divinity to the land and treat it as a friend, not an enemy.

They also found that their old religion was part of a larger religious system which once prevailed in other parts of the world as well. Nigel Pennick, author and thinker, found great similarity between old European Paganism and Hinduism. He said that Hinduism represented the Eastern expression of this universal tradition and foresaw the possibility that Hindus might come to accept Europe's Pagans as a European branch of Hinduism.

Prudence Jones, the spokesperson for the U.K. Pagan Federation, said the same things. She observed that all the world's indigenous and ethnic religions have three features in common: they are nature-venerating, seeing nature as a manifestation of

[6]Christianity conquered Europe "from above", but many parts still continued to be pagan for quite some time. The Baltic States, for example, were pagan till the time of the Crusades. These were eventually conquered by the Order of Knights Templars, initially formed to fight the Saracens.

Divinity; secondly, they are polytheistic and recognize many Gods, many Manifestations; the third feature is that they all recognize the Goddess, the female aspect of Divinity as well as the male. She showed how European Paganism was similar to Hinduism, Shintoism, and the North American tradition. She thought that apart from doctrinal similarity, it would be useful for the European Pagans to be affiliated with a world Hindu organization which would give them legal protection — remember, that Paganism in Europe is still a heresy and it has no legal rights and protection. She emphasized that European Pagan religion is the native, indigenous religion of Europe, and religions with doctrines like Christianity came later.

The Americas

Among the indigenous peoples of two Americas, there is a growing awareness of their old identity. The ancient New World has a great message to give to the new Old World; it has to tell us about the mystery of the Mother Earth, tell us that we not only come *to* the Earth but we also come *from* the Earth. But one wonders if it is articulate enough culturally and, in fact, if enough of its old authentic religious tradition still survives to become the basis of a new revival. Indigenous America is poor, deprived, demoralized and not conscious enough of its spiritual heritage. In Central and Southern America, where there is still considerable native population left, things are no better. They are by far under the tutelage of Christian priests and functionaries who have ruled the roost for centuries. Now these priests are opposed, sometimes even violently, by lay Christians, by Evangelists from the North, and by radical Christianity which calls itself Liberation Theology. But they are sides of the same coin, and it has brought no relief to indigenous religions.[7] Indigenous

[7]Norman Lewis in his *The Missionaries* (Secker.) tells us that the new missionaries are working in pretty the same old way, and that nothing has changed since the seventeenth-century Jesuits, except that that the new crusaders are equipped with planes, radios and refrigerators stocked with soft drinks. The very first story in the book, set in post-war Guatemala, tells us of an American Evangelist who tries to suppress Indian festivals and replace traditional Indian symbols on women's blouses with Disney

culture is as much opposed by the orthodox church as by the radical one. The former used to sell Jesus as a Saviour, the latter sells him as a liberator. The aim of both is the same: to keep indigenous America in cultural bondage. Old America will never rise politically unless it rises culturally and it revives its old religion.

Countries under Islam

The condition of countries now dominated by Islam is a difficult one. People here have yet to win the basic struggle for intellectual freedom. Once this is done, the rest would be a question of time. The people will be free to inquire into the dogmas of Islam, and look at the life and revelations of their Prophet more critically; they will also know more about other religious traditions including their own past religions. This may bring the necessary corrective and may even topple the Islamic apple-cart. Who knows that in not too distant future the awakened Arabs may not demand the restoration of their old Temple at Mecca which Muslims destroyed?

However, despite discouraging conditions for the time being, some advanced thinkers in Muslim countries have shown awareness of the fact that Islam was an imposition on their country. For example, Tawfiq al-Hakim, a well-known dramatist

---

animals. The author tells us of two organizations which lead the hunt for converts: The Summer Institute of Linguistics, which masquerades as an institute to study tribal languages, and The New Tribes Mission, which recruits less educated fundamentalists from the American Bible Belt. Missionaries in Bolivia and Paraguay are involved in rounding up the Ayoreo, one of the last nomadic peoples of forbidding Chaco. Many of the terrified 'savages' die in the process of being captured, and many lapse into prostituting their girls, but the self-appointed saviours take it all philosophically.

Lewis saw the worst missionary callousness and deviousness when he went to investigate atrocities against the Ache in Paraguay and the Panare in Venezuela. In each case, the villains were from The New Tribes Mission. The Ache were herded into mission compounds because 'Hell is where those who cannot be reached will spend eternity.' Unfortunately the Ache had no concept of hell. So they were told that 'A fire hotter than anything they could make is waiting for each one of them without Christ.' Similarly the Panare were told that 'God will exterminate the Panare by throwing them on the fire. It is a huge fire.'

and social thinker of Egypt, was writing in the twenties and the thirtees of this century on this subject. Quite understandably, he had to do it guardedly. He said that the "classical Arab", his name for Islam, was inadequate for "spiritual" Egypt, which he identified with Pharaonic golden age. He also found that Hinduism and Pharaonic Paganism of ancient Egypt were congruent and had been in contact. He thought that the responsibility for articulating a spiritual alternative to Europe's materialism lay on neo-Pharaonist Egypt and Hindu India. There is a highly informative and analytic article on the subject by Dennis Walker, a young Australian Arabist.

Iran, another ancient country which lost its individuality when it was conquered by Islam, also shows signs that it is aware of its "Aryan" past. But it has made two mistakes. First, it thought it could combine its pride in its ancient religion and culture with its present-day Islam; secondly, it underestimated the power of Ayatollahs, the fanatic Muslim priests. It has to realize that it cannot revive its religious and cultural individuality so long as Islam holds it down.

The African continent has been under the attack of the two monolatrous religions, Christianity and Islam, for centuries. Under this attack, it has already lost much of its old culture. Recently, the attack has very much intensified and indigenous Africa is almost on the verge of losing its age-old religions. Some time ago, there was an article in the London *Economist* praising it for taking this attack with such pagan *tolerance*. But there was no word of protest against intolerance practised against its peoples and their religions. Thanks to the powerful Missionary lobby in the United Nations, there is a Universal Declaration of Human Rights which states that everyone has a right to embrace the religion of his choice. But where is a similar Declaration which says that tolerant philosophies and cultures have a right to protect themselves against aggressive, systematic proselytizing ? Are its well-drilled legionaries, organized round a fanatic and totalitarian idea, to have a free field? Should not the Missionary Apparatus, a threat not only to Africa but to the whole Third World, be wound up? Has the UNO no obligation in this regard?

Within what is now known as the Indian Sub-continent and Greater India itself, Islam is very powerful. But there is no doubt that once Hinduism comes into its own and begins to speak for itself, those who were forced to leave it under very special circumstances will return to their old fold.

IX

Hinduism

Hinduism can help all peoples seeking religious self-renewal, for it preserves in some way their old Gods and religions;[8] it preserves in its various layers religious traditions and intuitions they have lost. Many countries now under Christianity and Islam had once great religions; they also had great Gods who adequately fulfilled their spiritual and ethical needs and inspired in them great acts of nobility, love and sacrifice. But for many centuries they have been under great attack and much has been said against them while they gracefully retired to give the new totalist deity a chance to give whatever it had to offer. The results have been disastrous. Religious bigotry descended upon the earth; the concept of "one" God brought in the concept of two humanities and religious aggression became the highest duty and morality. Religion itself became dogmatic and lost its inwardness and vision. People both individually and collectively felt empty inside.

Now in their search for meaning, many peoples are turning to their old Gods. But during the long period of neglect, they lost the knowledge which could revive those Gods. Hinduism can help them with this knowledge.

[8]This very fact gives some Missionaries great hopes. They feel that they can do to Hinduism what they did to old classical religions. The late Fr. J. Monchanin, the founder of Sacchidananda Ashram in Tiruchirapalli (now presided over by Fr. Bede Griffiths), and a Missionary of the De Nobili school, says that the problem of Christianizing India is "of the same magnitude as the Christianization, in former times, of Greece", and he finds that "the Christianization of Indian civilization is to all intents and purposes an historical undertaking comparable to the Christianization of Greece."

In its simplest aspect, Europeans can best study their old pre-Christian religion by studying Hinduism. It is possible because there was a time when the two peoples shared a common religious milieu. The *Encyclopaedia Britannica* says: "Celtic religion, presided over by Druids (the priestly order), presents beliefs in various nature deities and certain ceremonies and practices that are similar to those in Indian religion. They also shared certain similarities of language and culture, thus indicating an ancient common heritage." But the problem has also a deeper aspect which we have discussed in our *The Word As Revelation: Names Of Gods,* and into which we need not go here. Suffice it to say that in this book, we have shown that, spiritually speaking, monotheism has no natural superiority over polytheism and, in point of historical fact, it has been worse. We also said that Hinduism has still the knowledge of the archetypal spiritual consciousness which expresses itself in the language of Many Gods, and therefore can help countries which are seeking their lost Gods. We said that those Gods are not lost but have merely gone out of manifestation, and that they can reappear again if properly invoked; that it could be a rewarding pilgrimage if we journeyed back to them to make our heart's offerings.

We said that it will help the pilgrim nations in many ways. They have been taught to regard their past as a benighted period of their history, but a more understanding approach to their old Gods will make for a less severe judgement on their past and their ancestors. It will fill the generation gap, not the one we generally talk about, but the deeper one of historical rootlessness of nations. Gods provide an invisible link between the past and the present of a nation; when they go, the historical link also snaps. The peoples of Egypt, Iran, Greece, Germany, Scandinavian and Baltic countries are quite ancient but as they lost their Gods, they also lost their sense of historical identity.

We also said that what is true of Europe is also true of Africa and South America. The countries of these continents have recently gained political freedom, but it has done little to help them to regain their spiritual identity. If they wish to rise in a deeper sense, they must recover their soul, their Gods, their roots in their own psyche. If they need any change, and there is no doubt they do, it must come from within themselves as a part of their own experience. They have to make the best use of their own psychic and spiritual gifts. They cannot rise through imported deities, saviours and prophets.

X

Muir thought that comparative studies of Christianity and Islam and their founders would also yield an indirect benefit. Writing in the *Calcutta Review* in 1845, he said that as "the Hindu, sickened by idolatry (Islam's and Christianity's common name for Hinduism), turns to the other two religions which surround him, and inquires into their respective claims...we must be ready at hand to meet him with the proofs of our most holy faith... the comparison of the two religions, Christianity and Islam, cannot fail to be of essential service, under God's blessings, to lead to practical results."

Muir deserves our thanks for thinking so much of debates and "proofs" in establishing the superiority of his faith. This was a language quite new to Islam and until not long ago also to Christianity. It does not however appear that the Hindu was sickened by his own religion, and that he was impatient to join one of the two Semitic religions. But he had certainly been under a great barrage of attack of the two monolatrous religions, and anything which improved his level of information and education about them was a welcome development. Muir's book was and still is a great help to such Hindus who care to know more about the Prophet of Islam, and, indeed, about Islam itself — for no other creed is so synonymous with its founder. Voice of India, therefore, deserves our thanks for bringing out a reprint of Muir's *The Life of Mahomet* as it did a few years ago of D.S. Margoliouth's *Mohammed and the Rise of Islam*. That too carried our Introduction, in which we had discussed the importance of such studies for India and the need for her to develop her own scholarship and perspective. We had also pointed out that hitherto we have looked at Hinduism through the eyes of Islam and Christianity, but that it is high time that we now also learn to look at them through the eyes of Pagan religions in general and of Hinduism in particular. The two Introductions may best be read together.

THREE

SEMITIC RELIGIONS AND YOGIC SPIRITUALITY

What forcibly strikes a discriminating student of the Bible is that its god lacks interiority. Though the Bible exhorts its followers to love their god with all their heart, yet throughout its long career there is nothing to show that it knows of a "god or gods in the heart"; it shares this lack of interiority with the Quran too, its successor. Both however speak of a "god in heaven," showing that he enjoys an elevated status among his followers.

This god also lacks universality which suffered further contraction in connotation and denotation with the passage of time. Though initially the Jews and their neighbours had their own gods, but in many ways they were interchangeable and they could stand for each other. But with time, the biblical god became more and more particularistic. He became a special god of a chosen people. "I will take you to me for a people, and I will be to you a God," he said to the Jews and struck a special covenant with them. By the time Christianity and Islam appeared on the scene, this god had lost his interchangeability with other gods and his capacity to represent them and be represented by them. He was a god of a particular people and worked for and operated through them alone.

One can easily trace this development through the Bible. Abraham, belonging to the early biblical period, is a man of deep faith. He believes in his god implicitly and has even some sort of a covenant with him, but he knows that others too have their gods and he does not quarrel with this fact, and it does not occur to him to deny them. There is nothing wrong if a devotee exalts his god and if he feels he has a special relationship with him — all this happens often enough and is part of normal spirituality. But the trouble starts when it becomes the basis of a hate-campaign against the gods of one's neighbours. According to Hindu view, it comes from a *tāmasika-rājasika* faith.

According to certain traditions, Abraham revolted against the image worship of his forefathers, but there is nothing to show that it turned him into a regular iconoclast. It seems that he did not yet believe that the best way of showing his faith in his god was by breaking the images of the gods of his neighbours— that tradition was to begin later with Moses and other prophets. Nor does it seem that he eschewed every physical representation or token of divinity. For when he struck a covenant with his god, the latter told him to get all his male descendents circumcised to "show there is a covenant between you and me" (Gen. 17.12) — rather an unhappy representation and a grotesque way of memorializing a heavenly act.

Ruth, a lovable early character in the Bible, also illustrates this point. She was a Moabite young lady married to a young Jew whose family had settled in her homeland during years of famine in their own land. The young man died leaving her a widow. Her mother-in-law, a kindly lady, decided to go back to her own land. Ruth wanted to accompany her but she advised the young lady to stay back with her own "people and gods." But Ruth said: "Entreat me not to leave you or to return from following you; where you go I will go...Your people shall be my people, and your god will be my god; and where you die, I will die, and there will I be buried." Ruth belonged to a biblical period when "your gods" were recognized as valid gods, when gods were yet made for men and not men for gods, when loyalty to a god did not involve repudiation of loyalty and fellow-feelings in normal human relations, and when other people and other gods could be adopted.[1]

[1]Indeed, there is a whole section in the Old Testament which does not square with its dominant ideas. The Proverbs, to my mind the best part of the Bible, represents a non-Mosaic tradition. In its spirit, it is very different from the Pentateuch and the Prophets; its ethics is high; it represents a very different spiritual tradition, the tradition of Self-knowledge. Its teaching is mostly anonymous; it has also a woman teacher, a mother teaching ethical behaviour to her son (31), rather an exception in the Bible. It speaks of man, not of God's special people; it does not have a prophetic theme (covenant), and it makes no specific reference to Israel's faith; it has minimum of the biblical God in it. In it, the word "Adonai" does not occur at

There are many instances in the Old Testament to show that the ordinary Jewish people were not as exclusive as their prophets. They interacted with their neighbours, even borrowed and lent their gods and their rites and usages like other people; but their prophets laboured hard to keep them apart, and remain, as they said, a holy people. The cult of a god who stands in isolation and denied other gods began seriously enough with Moses. Foreign gods became "abominations or detestations" (Heb. *sheqets*). The subsequent prophetic tradition in the Bible continued it. Many prophets came and kept warning their followers against going astray, against going "a whoring after other Gods". But the common Jews were intractable and kept relapsing into wrongful ways of worship so much so that the Almighty was often led to declare: "How long will this people provoke me?" But eventually the prophets were successful and the Jews believed that they were a special people of a special god.

2. Messiah

By the time Jesus came the cult of a one god and a special people was well established. But he faced the problem of a plurality of Messiahs. During many centuries of foreign domination, the Jews had learnt to expect a Messiah, a religious-political personage, who was also to be their king and deliverer from the foreign bondage. His coming was to be preceded by many signs. Many claimed to be Messiahs from time to time but failed to clinch their claim. In fact, there was no way to decide and there was much uncertainty around. Even those like John the Baptist who proclaimed the coming Messiah were not sure. We are told that John after he had watched Jesus's appearance for considerable time began to doubt whether Jesus was the coming

all; the word, "Elohim," which occurs more than 2200 times in the rest of the Bible occurs only four times in this part. The word "Yahweh" (Lord) occurs somewhat more frequently (87 times) but it is small compared to 6855 times in the Bible. Though this portion has influenced the Talmud and the Mishna and other Jewish religious writings, it is unfortunate that Christianity and Islam drew their inspiration not from this source but from the Pentateuch and the Prophets.

one whom he had announced. He sent word by his disciples from his prison to Jesus: " Are you he who is to come, or shall we look for another?" (Mt.11.3). Later on, there was much controversy between the followers of John the Baptist and Jesus.

Though dogged by doubt, the hope for national independence however worked as a goad and the Jewish people were ready to try anyone who made the claim. But as the question had political implications it was neither safe for the claimants nor for the nation. The course brought them into collision with the Imperial authorities and invited oppression. Flavius Josephus (b. AD 37 or 38), the great Jewish historian, mentions several such Messiahs including Theudas who claimed ability to divide the Jordan river to allow his followers to pass dry-footed. But he was massacred by the Roman rulers along with his followers before he could prove his claim.

Just like many others when Jesus claimed to be the Messiah, he got an eager audience, particularly with his healing and miracles, all signs of a Messiah. But this very fact made the Jewish chiefs who were afraid of the Romans even more cautious. They met together and said: "What are we to do? For this man performs many signs. If we let him go on thus, every one will believe in him, and the Romans will come and destroy our holy place and our nation... it is expedient...that one man should die for the people, and that the whole nation should not perish" (Jn.11.47 ff).

And thus a good and innocent man died. But even this did not avert the tragedy for long, though the future events proved that the Jews had a point in attempting caution against their hotheads. Not long after Jesus, in AD 70, the Temple was burnt and the city of Jerusalem was levelled to the ground by Titus, the Roman general, for attempted rebellion.[2] A greater calamity

[2]Gibbon tells us how from the reign of Nero to that of Antoninus Pius, the Jewish impatience with Roman domination broke out in repeated massacres and insurrections, not only in Palestine but in all the Roman provinces where the Jewish population was significant; how these insurrections involved not only their Roman masters but also their fellow-subjects; and how when they could not take it on the Romans, they did it on their pagan neighbours. He tells us of the Jewish massacres "in the cities of Egypt, of

was to befall during the next century. One Bar-Kochkba claimed to be the Messiah-king of the Jews; he collected half a million fighting men, seized Jerusalem and held it for three years. But at the end, he was defeated. The Jews were turned out from the ruined city and forbidden to enter it on pain of death except on the ninth of Ab, the traditional anniversary of the destruction of the Temple when they could pay a tax and come to weep on the site of the old sanctuary. Ever since they have lived in dispersion in regions near or far away.

The city saw many conquerors before it finally passed into the hands first of Christians and then of Muslims and became their pilgrim centre. It is only now after a lapse of nineteen centuries, that the Jewish people are again able to reconstruct a national home for themselves in Palestine against great odds.[3]

3. From a Messiah to a Saviour

Jesus began as a Messiah of his people, or at least this is what he was taken for by them initially. He also tried to fit the role. He said that he had come not to abolish the law and the prophets but to fulfil them (Mt. 5.17,18), and that he was sent

---

Cyprus, and of Cyrene, where they dwelt in treacherous friendship with the unsuspecting natives....In Cyrene they massacred 220,000 Greeks; in Cyprus 240,000; in Egypt a very great multitude. Many of these unhappy victims were sawed asunder, according to a precedent to which David had given the sanction of his example."

[3]But though Jerusalem was lost, the hope of a Messiah remained. The one who made a considerable impact on Jewry was in the seventeenth century. Shabbathai Sebi, born in Smyrna around 1621 claimed to be the Messiah and drew wide attention throughout the Jews of the Middle East and Europe. Meanwhile, a young Polish Jewish lady also claimed that she was intended to be the wife of the Messiah. Shabbathai invited her to Cairo and married her. Then he moved to Constantinople, not without first dividing the kingdom of the earth among his chief followers. At Constantinople, he was arrested by the officers of the Sultan of Turkey. Sensing danger to his life, he converted to Islam. This pleased the Sultan very much and he appointed him as one of his doorkeepers. He lost his prestige among the Jews but not before he put their life again in jeopardy. The Jews were not lucky in their Messiahs. Jesus had already brought them under a great misfortune. They had become victims of hatred and pogroms of the very followers of one who once claimed to be their Messiah, who was to bring them liberation. History moves in strange ways.

to "the lost sheep of the house of Israel" (Mt. 15.24). He charged his preachers to "go nowhere among the Gentiles, and enter no town of the Samaritans" (Mt. 10.5,6); he preached that "salvation is from the Jews" (Jn. 4.22); he said that his teaching was for the Jews, that they "be first fed," and that it was "not right to take the children's (Jews') bread and throw it to the dogs" (non-Jews) (Mk.7.27).

But when this role failed, Jesus presented himself in another garb. When Jews rejected him, he rejected the Jews. He told them that they had the Devil for their father (Jn. 8.44). He told them that as they were repudiating him, God, his Father, was repudiating them. He told them the parable of the householder who planted a vineyard: how when the tenants disobeyed and rebelled against the master's servants and even his son, they were turned out and the vineyard was let out to others (Mt. 21.33-41). He declared that God was terminating his old covenant with the Jews, and entering into a new one with those who believed in His Son. He asked his disciples to "let the children come", his name for the Gentiles. Christians replaced Jews as God's chosen people; the latter were now redundant in God's scheme but they were to be tolerated by the Church until all mankind had been converted to Christianity and the Jewish testimony was no longer needed. Jesus himself was converted from a Messiah into a Saviour, into God's First Begotten Son, the Intermediary between God and man. This indeed was a great leap and a great promotion from the humble figure of a Jewish Messiah.

Borrowings

But this transformation did not happen in a day; it took quite some time and at the back of it lay several centuries of borrowings from non-Judaic sources. When Christianity began to break away from its old moorings and sought a new audience, it found itself faced with several competitors with whom it lustily engaged in a game of one-upmanship. It went on a spree of unacknowledged borrowing and stealing. There were too many Saviours around. They were often born on a particular day, lived under similar circumstances, and they invariably rose after dying. Jesus's title and life as a Saviour followed the current fashion. For example, Mithra, the founder of Mithraism, a creed which had gone to the Roman world from Persia and was already well-known when Christianity appeared on the scene, was born on or very near the 25th of December, of a Virgin Mother and in a cave; after he was buried he rose from the tomb; he had twelve disciples and the members of his order were admitted with the ceremony of baptism; he was also called a Saviour. Jesus's life was made to follow the pattern and reproduce the circumstances in which other Saviours lived, died and rose.

Indeed, the Dying God and his Resurrection were popular themes in many ancient legends of the region. Archaeology has discovered old tablets which show a passion play of Baal, Babylon's Sun-God, which probably Jews had often seen during the days of their captivity. It provided the pattern for the lives of many gods and saviours including Jesus. His life as given in the Gospels is so true to the current pattern that many scholars wonder whether it is a biography at all. The current Jewish history mentions no Jesus. The Talmud mentions one Jeschu ben Pandira who was crucified but that had happened a hundred years before the Christian era.

Because of these facts, many scholars regard Jesus's life closer to legend than to history, and whether there was any historical Jesus at all is a much-discussed question in the scholarly world. But the question is losing its old importance and many Christian theologians have now begun to talk of a Jesus of faith rather than of history. Perhaps, they have come to realize in the heart of their hearts that insistence on a historical Christ is a form of idolatry. However, changing the format does not change the nature of the question and does not take it out from the purview of rationality. The question still remains whether a gratuitous faith based on the figure of a saviour imagined or historical (Soul cares for a psychic reality, not a historical presence— Gita 2.16) is rationally or spiritually tenable. A little reflection will show that it offends man's rational as well as his spiritual sensibility.

Christianity borrowed not only the figure of a Saviour but also most of its central rites from the creeds and mystery cults current at the time in Egypt, Syria, and the Mediterranean world. Almost all its important rites are embarrassingly similar to theirs', though early Christian fathers had no difficulty in accounting for this similarity. Justin Martyr said that the Devil had anticipated and introduced into the religion of Mithra usages similar to those of Christians. Later on, Tertullian came out with the same kind of explanation in connection with the Lord's Supper and said that the pagan "devils whose business is to prevent the truth, mimic the exact circumstances of the divine sacraments in the mysteries of the idols."

Thus Christianity borrowed from two sources: Judaic and non-Judaic. It borrowed from Judaism its scripture, its prophets, its belief in a special people and a special covenant, and above all its jealous God, its hatred for 'other' Gods, and consequently its proverbial hatred of mankind—misotheosy is the parent of misanthropy. It also borrowed the idea of Atonement through a blood sacrifice from the same source. These ideas were core ideas and had a great influence in shaping its subsequent ethos. But it has also some non-Judaic sources for some of its other equally important ideas like the Saviour, the Virgin Birth, Resurrection, the Lord's Supper.[4] Its own contribution was that the God of its special covenant began to claim universal sovereignty, its saviour began to claim to save all, and it itself claimed a world mission. Its other contributions were the Cross, the Hell, the Devil, possession and exorcism.[5] They were by no means

[4]Several scholars like R. Seydel, R. Garbe, A.J. Edmunds, Van Eysinga have also spoken of Indian contribution. Many believe that Simeon (Lk. 2.23-35), Temptation, Peter's Walking on Water, Miracles of Loaves have been taken from Buddhist sources. Probably the significant borrowings were in the field of ethics through the channel of the Essenes, but as these ethical teachings became part of a very different belief-system, they lost much of their shaping influence.

[5]The Devil is definitely a New Testament contribution. In the Old Testament the word occurs only 4 times, but in the New Testament it occurs 109 times and plays an important part. Devils were the first to recognize Jesus for what He was (Mk. 1.24; 3.11). Similarly, in the Old Testament there is hardly any reference to demon-possession, but the Gospels abound in such

unimportant; in fact, Christianity's history cannot be understood without them, but we shall not discuss them here.

Judaism taught remission of sin by sacrifice, preferably of one's first-born; but it added that God in his mercy accepted a substitute. Christianity raised the idea of sin, a blood sacrifice and the vicarious atonement to new heights and built an elaborate theology round it. It believed that "without shedding of blood is no remission" (Heb. 9.22); but it added that Jesus, not only the first-born but the only begotten son of God, made this sacrifice for all mankind once for all by shedding his blood. The cross is central to Christianity. All before leads up to it and all after looks back to it. After making sin into a formidable dogma, its remission is made simple enough—just baptism in the name of the Father, the Son and the Holy Ghost. Sin is no more a problem for the followers of Jesus. It has already been atoned for by him.[6] As an Anglican Hymn (633) puts it:

There is a fountain filled with Blood
Drawn from Emmanuel's veins,
And sinners plunged beneath that flood
Lose all their guilty stains.

4. Prophet

A Messiah was a phenomenon of late Judaism. In fact, the word occurs only two times in the Old Testament, and it had a

---

cases. When Jesus sent out his apostles, he "gave them power and authority over all devils, and to cure diseases" (Lk. 9.1). In fact, in the first three centuries, Christians were regarded as natural exorcists. The Church of Rome has always had an Order of exorcists. The Greek and Roman writers hardly mention evil demons but early writings of Christian Fathers and saints are full of them. Christian John Cassian of early fifth century says that "the air between heaven and earth is so crammed with Spirits... that it is fortunate for men that they are not permitted to see them." John Wesley, the founder of the Methodist Church, says that "giving up witchcraft is in effect giving up the Bible." In the long history of Christianity, devils and demons have played a great role.

[6]Mahatma Gandhi recalls his early contacts with Plymouth Brethren in South Africa. One of them proclaimed that "as we believe in the Atonement of Jesus, our sins do not bind us." Gandhi says that the man was "as good as his words," and he "committed transgressions," but remained "undisturbed by them."

secular rather than a religious connotation. The central idea in the biblical Judaism was a prophet who warned, predicted and proclaimed. Though Moses was a prophet par excellence, there was nothing exclusive about him. Anybody who had the reputation of being moved by the "spirit of the Lord" was called a prophet, and therefore we have many prophets in the Old Testament; in fact, at this time, the prophetic skill was often cultivated in certain schools. Nor was a prophet unique to the Jews. Their neighbours had their own prophets who were even consulted by Jewish princes.

But with time, the idea of prophet took a new turn. It was not enough that God talked to you; the equally important thing was that he did not talk to anyone else. Christianity's propagation of 'the only Saviour' created a demand and a market for the idea of 'the only Prophet' as well. To be a prophet, one among many, was no longer much of a feather in one's cap. One had to be a special prophet, a prophet with a difference in order to count; he had also to have a world mission.

Thus Muhammad came at a time when it was not enough to be *a* prophet; he had to be *the* prophet. He was surrounded by Jews and Christians who already had their Prophets and Saviours and displayed them proudly. Muhammad began boldly but cautiously. He first said that the same God talked to him who talked to Abraham, Moses and Jesus, and that he came with the same message with which they did. But when he found that Christians and Jews did not take him seriously, he increased his claim. He declared that he was the most authentic spokesman of God up to his time and also for all time to come as well, that he was the seal of prophecy, that through him religion was now finally made perfect, and that any old revelation was now redundant and a new one presumptuous.

The claim was initially not entertained even by the Arabs; but, in the end, Muhammad was able to get it established through the display of superior force. Now, among the Muslims, it is a part of their creed and even to question it is a crime. The *shariat* prescribes death penalty for denying Muhammad's Prophethood or 'defiling' his name in any way. One could even defile his name indirectly by giving up Islam or by claiming some sort of prophethood for oneself. This invites death both by the jury as well as the mob and the assassins' hands.[7]

Mirza Ghulam Ahmad (1835–1905), the founder of the Qadiani or Ahmadiya sect, though otherwise quite a fanatic Muslim, however claimed to be a *mujaddid*, a Renewer of Islam. This brought his sect in unanticipated conflict with orthodox Muslim opinion. Recently one Muhammad Sharif Ahmad Amini, a spokesman of this sect, said that during the last few years in Pakistan four Ahmadiyas were sentenced to death, four to life imprisonment, and forty-eight including a woman were killed. They are not allowed to call themselves Muslims, give "*azān*", or say "*salām 'alaikum*" (*The Statesman*, 26th October, 1987). Reports have also come from such unlikely places as Canada where Ahmadiyas have been assassinated by secret Muslim bands out to enforce Muhammad's claim as the "seal of prophets" (*khātimu'n-Nabīyīn*).

More Saviours and Prophets

But in spite of inhibitive and repressive circumstances in which would-be saviours and prophets often work, they have not ceased to exist. The phenomenon is not something which happened only in old days or during the medieval times; claims continued to be made even in more recent times and, what is more important, they were also believed. True, they were not successful stories like those of Moses or Jesus or Muhammad, but they were not without their audience. One prominent case was that of Richard Brothers (1757–1824), a half-pay officer of

[7]Such threats however have only inhibited but not stopped people from making similar claims though they have done it cautiously and in a guarded language. They have claimed to be *walis*, or *imāms*, or *qutbs* (axis, or pole); like the final prophet, they have claimed to be the final (*al-tamm*) *imāms*; like the prophet who claimed to be the "seal of prophecy" (*khātimau'n-nabūwah*), they have claimed to be the seal of sanctity (*khātim al-wilāyah*). Some have claimed the status of a "silent" prophet (*sammit*), perhaps implying that Muhammad was merely a *natiq*, a speaking prophet. But all of them have taken care to shout louder than others their protestation of fealty to the Prophet while they made their claims. It was a wise precaution, but it did not always save them from the wrath of Muslim theologians.

the British Navy, who claimed to be a divinely appointed prophet. He described himself as a "nephew of the Almighty," and claimed his descent from David. Though he was confined as a lunatic, but he could count many distinguished people amongst his followers.

We may also mention two similar movements in the USA: Southcottians and the Mormons. The leader of the first was a lady, Joanna Southcott (1750–1814). She claimed to be the woman chosen by God to appear at the end of ages. As man's Fall came through woman, his salvation was also to come through her. She claimed she was "pregnant with Shiloh", probably some expected Messiah, but unfortunately she died before she could deliver. One of her disciples, George Turner, prophesied that the Lord would come in 1817 and rule the world; he even named the Lord's cabinet and their salaries in advance. He said that the Lord would "increase a hundred-fold the power of men and women to enjoy each other," anticipating India's Rajaneesh by over a hundred and fifty years.

The leader of the second movement was Joseph Smith (1805–1844), founder of The Church of Jesus Christ of Latter-Day Saints, commonly called Mormons. He claimed that he was ordained to Aaronic priesthood by John the Baptist, to Melchizedek priesthood by Peter, James and John, receiving Holy Apostleship and the keys of the Kingdom with power to seal on earth so that it might be sealed in heaven. All these claims did not tax the credulity of his followers and the Mormons are now a flourishing community in the USA.

We have a similar case in Mirza Ali Muhammad, the founder of Babism. He first claimed to be the "Manifestation" or *Bāb* (the Gate) between the Hidden Imam and his followers. But later on, he found this title too humble and while bestowing it on one of his disciples, he himself assumed the title of *Nuqtā*, "the Point". Later came his more famous disciple now known to the world under the adopted name of Bahaullah (Splendour of God). He claimed to be the true Manifestation, while his teacher, Ali Muhammad, was only a harbinger of his advent, a kind of John the Baptist, and "in the blaze of the light of the New Day, the candle lit by Mirza Ali Muhammad ceased to merit attention, and, indeed, became invisible." His followers, the Bahais, are now doing well, particularly in America and even more so in India. In all these cases the lives of the founders of these sects were hardly edifying, but this did not come in the way of their finding a considerable audience.

Not long ago, one Hung Hsu-chuan, a Chinese convert to Christianity, a leader of the Taiping Rebellion, claimed to be the second son of Mary. He said that "the Father and the Elder Brother (Jesus) have descended upon earth and have taken me and the junior Lord (his own son) to regulate the affairs pertaining to the world. Father, Son and Grandson are together Lord of the New Heaven."[8] He established a new celestial dynasty and a new Trinity of the Father, the Son and the Grandson. One can only speculate what would have happened had Jesus married. Probably the Grandson would have replaced the Holy Ghost in the Trinitarian theology.

These latter-day prophets we have cited here sound laughable, yet they are not very different in principle from the preceding ones except that they did not succeed to the same extent. In fact, it is success which has made the difference between the two. Success is a great argument; it makes feasible what is otherwise ludicrous. Yet they both represent the same principle; they both represent prophetic spirituality; they both claim to be sole mouthpiece of God or his apostle or both. They can hardly claim any special moral or spiritual merit for the role they claim.

5. Exclusive Revelation

Why were they in particular chosen for certain roles? Why were certain things revealed to them which were kept hidden from others before? Had they some special moral or spiritual

[8]Hung told the visiting British Minister, Sir George Bonham, that he was the "Sovereign of the entire earth under the mandate of God." This is the worst part of some of these Eastern converts. When they adopt Christianity, they pretend to a direct relationship with God or his Son and begin to speak of their own mandate. Keshub Chandra Sen of India did the same though in a low key and offered to lead European Christianity. Surely, this cannot be acceptable to their European mentors.

qualities to qualify for these roles?

Most prophets have made their claims without trying to justify them. They must have found them so self-evident. Islam has not even raised the question; and it is certain it would not like a discussion of such questions at all. In a way, it has done us good and spared us from much sophistry. Christian theology, which is more trained in this line, has given us an answer. From their answer, we find that they understand the word Revelation in a special sense.

In its ordinary dictionary sense, the word Revelation means "unveiling something hidden," it means both the making known of something secret, and also truths thus made known. In this sense, the word has meanings of wide application. Things unknown to us are being revealed to us by others, and even we are discovering new things every time. We experience new things we had not known before, or we become conscious of things of which we have been hitherto unconscious. We also apply the word to things known to one part of the mind but now made known to another part. The word will also apply to things known to a deeper layer of mind, or to the secret knowledge of the soul of which we become aware through certain spiritual disciplines. Here it means that 'unmanifest' things become manifest. It is in this sense that the word is largely used in Hinduism, but other meanings are also legitimate and conform to our experience everywhere.

In prophetic religions, however, the word does not apply to anything so permissive and diffused; there it has a semi-technical meaning. According to the understanding of Christian theologians, the word means that activity of God by which "He took Noah, Abraham, and Moses, into his confidence, telling them what He had planned and what their part in His plan was to be" (J.I. Packer in *The New Bible Dictionary*); it culminated in the Revelation to Jesus who told us "all things that I heard of my father" (Jn.15.15). According to the *Dictionary*, this was "God's crowning and final revelation."

One may object that it all sounds arbitrary. But we are told, piously enough, by H.L. Goudge that "it belongs to God to reveal Himself when and how He will. If He reveals Himself to one nation more fully than to another, that belongs to God's "management of His household" (Eph.1.10). It was not for the lack of trying that other nations "knew not God" (1 Cor. 1.21), nor was it for any special virtue that the Jews were chosen as God's special people and God's purpose kept hidden from others was revealed to them. It was as he willed. God's "mystery which was kept secret for long ages" was now being "disclosed" for the first and the last time "according to the command of the eternal God" (Rom.16.25 ff). Revelation begun with biblical prophets "culminates in Christ and the Spirit-bearing Church" as H.L. Goudge puts it.

As usual, Christian theology has used pious language to reach an arrogant conclusion. "I thank thee, O Father, Lord of Heaven and earth, that thou didst hide these things from the wise and understanding, and didst reveal them into babes" (Mt. 11.25f), says the Bible with apparent piety but with great satisfaction. The claim is at heart boastful but, looked at from another angle, it has a certain kind of truth of its own. Christianity has only cared for a God known by babes and sinners; it has hardly an idea of a God revealed to wisdom, understanding and purity. In the Gnostic writings, *buddhi* or wisdom is not a dirty word as it is in Semitic scriptures. In the Upanishads, God is *buddhi-grāhyam*, that is he is revealed to purified *buddhi*; he is known by the pure, the wise, the understanding. God may belong to sinners as well, but he is known, so far as that is possible, only by those who have left sinning, the *apahatapāpman*. In the Upanishadic tradition, God's best introduction is not that he is 'the God of sinners', but that he is a destroyer of evil and sin; one of his most celebrated names is *pāpanāśana*, or *aghna*. Similarly, in the Indian tradition, he is more celebrated as a protector of the good (*paritrāṇāya sādhūnām*) than as a friend of 'publicans and sinners'. God is merciful to all, but certainly he is not a guardian of criminals of a nation enjoying extra-territorial treaty rights as they did during the last centuries when Europe and the Missionaries ruled the roost.

Christians are very snobbish about being sinners as communists have been about being proletarian. To be sinful has become a cult with them. To call a Christian sinful is complimentary to him. He resents being told otherwise. Paul was the "foremost of sinners," and he "received mercy for this reason" (1Tim.1.15f). The Christian heaven has more joy over one sinner who repents than over ninety-nine righteous persons who need no repentance (Lk.15.7). In fact, Christianity has more interest, almost a morbid interest as we shall see, in repentance than in righteousness.

6. Worship

Every religion has its own forms and modes of worship, both public and private, informed by its dominant ideas of God and man. Prophetic religions take great pride in "one" God, but it seems they have not found it always easy to handle him. In Christianity, he frankly became triune at a very early stage. Theoretically the three members were equal and in some way one but in practice they became separate and Jesus became more equal than the other two. In a later development, the Son replaced the Father, and in due course, the Son himself was replaced by the Mother, Mary, who was not even a member of the Trinity. There was yet another shift; saints and martyrs replaced them all. Their shrines and graves became paramount objects of worship. *The Ecclesiastical Cyclopaedia* gives us some illustrative, interesting statistics. It tells us that at Canterbury, the devotion towards St. Thomas Beckett (where his bones were translated to a new chapel in the Cathedral of Canterbury) quite effaced the adoration of the Deity. "At God's altar, for instance, there were offered in one year 3 pounds 2s. 6d.; at the Virgin Mary's, 63 pounds, 5s. 6d.; at St. Thomas's, 832 pounds 12s. 3d. But the next year the disproportion was still greater. There was not a penny offered at God's altar; the Virgin's gained only pound 4, 1s. 8d.; but St. Thomas had got for his share 954 pounds 6s. 3d."

The dead saints were far more useful than living ones, and their corpses even more so. Aldous Huxley tells us that during the middle ages, persons dying in the odor of sanctity ran the risk, when their bodies lay in state, of being stripped naked, or even dismembered by the faithful. Clothing would be cut to ribbons, ears cropped, hair pulled out, toes and fingers amputated, nipples snipped off and carried home as amulets. St. Romuald of Ravenna, visiting France, heard that the people proposed to kill him to have the members of his body as relics. When Saint Thomas Aquinas fell ill and died in the monastery of Fossanuova, where he had stopped while on a journey, the monks decapitated him and boiled his body to make sure of keeping his bones. There were open thefts, piracy and even wars between towns for the possession of dead bodies of saints, real or imagined. Relics were also faked. In all this there was hardly any God-worship. It was all worship of relics and graves. Relics were sought as amulets, as charms, as objects of worship. The churches abounded in them. One church in Rome displayed the following: Three pieces of the cross by which Jesus was hung in a case of gold. One of the holy nails with which Jesus was crucified. Two thorns from the crown of Jesus. One of the coins supposed to have been given for betrayal of Jesus. The cord by which Jesus was bound to the cross. A phial full of the blood of Jesus. A phial full of milk from the breast of Virgin Mary. Far away in Glasgow, a church possessed the mouth of St. Ninian in a golden casket; part of the zone of the blessed virgin; a small phial containing a portion of her milk. In France, Voltaire counted six foreskins of Jesus to which barren women made pilgrimage. The relics made for fertile trade and their supply never failed to keep pace with their demand. We learn from Calvin that there was so much wood in the relics of the Cross that not even three hundred men could carry them. Similarly, the Virgin's milk was aplenty. San Bernardino of Siena tells us that: "All the buffalo cows of Lombardy would not have as much milk as is shown about the world." R.W. Southern, author of *Western Society and the Church in the Middle Ages*, says that if we were able to draw up statistics of imports into England during this period, relics would certaily come high on the list.

Now all this has been regularized and systematized by the Catholic Church. The relics are certified by the Church authorities. A reliquary and a certificate of authentication are always entombed in the mensa of the altar of any new church or cathedral.

In Islam too, we find a lot of 'grave worship'. The Black Stone at Ka'ba is an object of worship. Umar thought that it was no more than a piece of stone but since the Prophet had worshipped it he also did the same. Every Muslim pilgrim runs between Safa and Marwa, "among Allah's waymarks," as the Quran calls them. In some places, the prophet's hair (*hazrat bāl*) is an object of great veneration.

One may not prefer this form of worship and adoration, yet is it more superstitious than the other kind of liturgy which takes the form of a theological formula and declares that a particular God alone is true and that some one is his begotten Son or Last Prophet? The latter may conform to a dogma or to *sunna*, but does it conform to the truth of the Spirit? Protestantism and Wahabism are as soulless as the practices they pretend to 'reform'. One is *tāmasika* and the other is *rājasika* worship but both lack elements of a *sāttvika* worship.

Vincet Smith finds that the "veneration of relics seems to be practically unknown to Brahmanical Hindus," but he finds nothing creditable in it, certainly no higher conception of worship. As he says it is simply due to the fact that "their ill-defined religion has no recognized founder like Jesus Christ, Buddha or Muhammad."

7. Spiritual Praxis

Apart from formal temple worship, aesthetic or grotesque, simple or complicated, most religions also prescribe certain spiritual practices to help their followers to realize the truths they preach. The *praxis* or what Hindus call *sādhanā* is shaped by the way a religion intuits God, man and nature. Religions like Hinduism and Buddhism prescribe a regimen of discipline known as *śila, samādhi,* and *prajñā,* to open up higher consciousness. They believe that even with all the guidance and help, each individual has to rediscover the spiritual truths for himself, that unless they are so done they can be of no use for him. One cannot eat or clothe by proxy; how can one live spiritual truths by proxy?

But as prophetic religions believe that God has already chosen them for no rhyme or reason and already revealed to them truths hidden from others, so what do they want any *sādhanā* for? They already know the truth and they have nothing for themselves to learn. Prophetic religions prescribe only certain beliefs and the religious duty to convert others to those beliefs through preaching and holy wars.

"Speaking with tongues"

It is therefore not strange that we find very little by way of *sādhanā* in the New Testament. One of these rare spiritual practices was known as "speaking with tongues." According to this practice, the believers gathered together in their churches, and waited on the Holy Ghost to descend upon them and speak through them (1 Cor. Chapter 14). As was to be expected, it led to a pandemonium. People under the influence of the so-called Holy Ghost talked unintelligibly and all at the same time. Even Paul who prescribed this method for his followers had to chide them. He asked them to speak in a language others understood and one at a time. He of course forbade women from speaking at all, for "did they think that the word originated with them, or they were the only ones it has reached?" He further added that it was "shameful for a woman to speak in a church," and that if there was anything they desired to know, "let them ask their husbands at home." And he ended by saying that if others thought they were true prophets, they should know that what he was saying was "a command of God," and that he who did not recognize this, "he himself is not recognized" (I Cor. 14.34 ff). Most of the time, these phenomena arise from self-suggestion and make-believe. But in more extreme cases, they border on abnormality. Cases of interior audition and automatic speech crop up from time to time. Modern Psychology tells us of cases of 'multiple personalities' where one 'personality' takes over, acts and speaks, without the other usual, normal personality knowing about it.

Repentance

The New Testament's other important teaching is to "repent, for the kingdom of heaven is at hand" (Mt. 4.17; 3.2). This teaching is repeated several times and may be called the cornerstone of the biblical teaching. The teaching about repentance has to be taken in conjunction with the Bible's other teachings about sin, its remission by sacrifice, and its once-for-all atonement by the blood of Jesus.

We know what havoc their combination wrought throughout the career of Christianity. The cults of sin and repentance reinforced each other. They led to their other sister-cults: the threat of Hell-fire, Purgatory, Indulgences. All this could not be healthy either for the mind or the soul and all was God-eclipsing. It veritably created a religion of what has been appropriately termed "spiritual terrorism."

It led to many negative features and gave rise to much neurotic, masochistic-sadistic behaviour. Atonement of sin by self-flagellation became widely common from the 11th century onward. Discipline of the scourge was in great repute. Clergy, laity, peasants and princes, men and women vied with each other in their devotion to the expiating lash, rod, thong, whip and chain-scourge. Princes got themselves flogged by their father confessors; in monasteries, they lashed themselves and lashed each other. Anything but amendment of life. Three thousand strokes and the chanting of thirty psalms expiated the sins of a year; thirty thousand strokes atoned for the offense of ten years, and so on in proportion. Wisdom, enlightenment, opening up of higher consciousness were altogether unknown to this species of spirituality.

Whole multitudes of men and women occasionally came out in the street, walked in procession, sometimes in thousands, moving from village to village, whipping themselves and indulging in what they called the "baptism of blood." They became a public nuisance and sometimes they were burnt to death by authorities, no fewer than ninety-one of them on one occasion in 1414 at Sangerhausen, for example. These throngs of men moved from place to place scourging themselves, celebrating and imitating the suffering of Christ, not forgetting to give a call for the killing of Jews as a task most meritorious and most pleasing to God. In all this there was a lot of Christian-style piety and devotion, but very little spirituality.

8. Iconoclasm

While discussing spiritual praxis of prophetic religions, we cannot leave out their iconoclasm, the most prominent *sādhanā* they have preached and practised. They have believed that demolishing the images on an altar, particularly in the temples of their neighbours, is the best way of worshipping their God and it is the service most acceptable to him. The impeccable hostility towards 'other' Gods is the most important part of their *sādhanā*.

There have been many religious cultures which did not build imposing shrines and made much use of images as the word is ordinarily understood in their system of worship. But they were by no means 'image-breakers'. Vedic Hindus had no temples though they had rich religious symbology. But this did not make them iconoclasts, nor it made them deny 'other' Gods. On the other hand, they admitted many Names and many approaches and concluded that it is the "same Reality which the wise call by many names," that he is Aryamā, he is Rudra, he is the Great God, he is Agni, he is Sūrya, he is the great Yama." Image-breaking is a contribution of prophetic religions.

Idols were used in most religiously rich countries. They were used by Egyptians, Chaldeans, Greeks, Hindus, Buddhists, by Mexican and Peruvians, the most developed cultures in the Americas; on the other hand, they were conspicuous by their absence among most primitive tribes. Bushmen, Eskimos, Hottentots, primitive societies of America had no use for them. G. d'Alviella writing on the subject quotes the authority of an early writer Lafitan who says: "We may say in general that the majority of savage people have no idols." A good deal of religious reflection must take place before images are used in worship. In India, the outer images were most often contributed by men who practised most advanced internal disciplines. These were 'icons', internal realities expressed in outer forms so far as that is possible.

Christians have idols in thousands in their churches as in St. Peter's in Rome and St. Paul's in London; they are representational and there is not even an attempt to give them an iconic form. As a result, while in a Hindu temple matter has been etherealized, in churches it is even more solidified. If you visit them, you are filled with the materiality of it all.

Why are prophetic religions so hostile to images? Is it because they have such a lofty idea of their god that they detest all his representations? It does not seem so. For they detest representations of even his creatures. They say that idols are powerless, dumb, deaf, blind. They are called 'futile', 'nothing', 'dung-pellets' *(gillulim)*. Then why are they so afraid of them? The idols seem to have more attraction for and more power over iconoclasts than over the worshippers. What else will account for iconoclasts' obsessive hatred of them? What imaginary goblin or spectre could excite such unreasonable dread and opposition? The fact is that in their heart they regard the idols *real* and so powerful that even their god is set at nought by them. They are so powerful that they have kept Semitic prophets on their toes and busy demolishing them—some kind of idolatry or fetish worship in reverse.

Denying an image or symbol on the altar for the reason that it is not god is not even bright. For it does not take much perspicacity to see that the two are different. Nobody confuses the picture of a friend with the friend himself. Nor does anyone think, unless he is neurotic, that he enhances the reality of his friend or his own friendship in any way by destroying his picture.

The fact is thc prophetic religions have not reflected deeply on the difference between form and the formless, between what is material and what is spiritual. The material view has so much occupied their mind that they are incapable of going beyond and see the incorporeal behind the corporeal. Their view of their god himself is external, so how can they be expected to have a more internal view of his image? Through spiritual awakening some have turned idols into Gods; others of unawakened soul have turned Gods into idols.

No great harm is done if we give our gods human eyes and ears and hands, but it is sheer disaster to give them human passions, human hatreds and preferences. Anthropomorphic gods are no problem; the fearful things are anthropopathic gods. Prophetic religions have given their God all human weakness and passions; on the other hand, Hinduism has thought of man with all divine virtues. The former have deified God, the latter have deified man.

Hinduism has reflected a lot on the problem. The Upanishads have their own iconoclasm, but that is of a spiritual nature. They say, Not this, Not this, even to most subtle forms. They also however affirm progressively deeper and more luminous forms, and say, This also is That, This also is That. Their God is the very form of truth, *tapas* and knowledge; He is *satya-svarūpa, tapa-svarūpa, vijñāna-svarūpa.*

Semitic style of iconoclasm is a child of crass materialism; it comes from incapacity to see that the physical is also the standing ground of the metaphysical; it comes from one's inability to see life, consciousness and divinity in things. Spiritual realities cannot be seen without inner, spiritual development. The capacity to see the incorporeal in the corporeal and the stable in the unstable (*a-śarīram śarīreshu* and *an-avastheshu-avasthitam*—Kaṭhopnishad) does not belong to all. Some people don't have the Gods within and are not ready yet, but they complain against the images outside. They don't see the idols within them but they quarrel with the idols on the altar. According to the Yogas, it is the spiritual mind that sees spiritual realities; it sees them in and beyond the visible material forms. The Upanishads speak of "the golden Person seen within the sun" (*antar āditye hiraṇmayaḥ purushaḥ*);[9] they speak of "Him who dwells in the sun, yet is other than the sun, whom the sun does not know, whose body the sun is."[10] The Atharvaveda

[9](Chhānd Up 1.6.6)

[10]*ya āditye tishṭhannādityād antaraḥ, yam ādityo na veda, yasyādityaḥ śarīram* (Brihad Up 3.7.9).

speaks of the sun "which all see with their eyes but not all know with their mind."[11] Plato, far away in Greece, says precisely the same thing in his *Laws*, that "everyone sees the body of the sun, but no one sees his soul," though this soul is "better than the sun," and "ought by every man to be deemed a God." It needs a certain development in one's own soul before he sees it around him.

Hindu spirituality teaches us that "all this is filled with God"[12] (Plato says, "All things are full of Gods"); that all is astir with life, consciousness and divinity. The Upanishads see "the earth, the atmosphere, the heaven, the waters, the mountains meditating as it were."[13] After such a vision, who can approach nature without reverence? It is not only higher spirituality, it is also proper ecology.

Hindu scriptures also say that God is formless and only our knowledge of him has form. The Yogas say that the Gods become truly formless when our mind becomes formless. The problem of prophetic religions is not that their god is formless, but that he has a rigid, stiff form which cannot take on and reflect other forms.

Christianity and Islam have engaged in large-scale destruction of temples of others through centuries. Both have thought that to serve their God they have to demolish the temples of the their infidel neighbours and demolish the images of their Gods. And this is enough. They need not know the idols in their own heart.

9. The Theology of Missions and *Jihād*

Every religion has its own ethos. The ethos is shaped by the kind of questions raised and the answers given by the leaders of that religion. In Hinduism, the seeker raised the question: What is real? What is the highest Good? What is man? What are his

[11]*pashyanti sarve chakshushā na sarve mansā viduḥ* (Ath Veda 10.8.14).
[12]Īśopnishad 1.
[13]*dhyāyatīva prithivī, dhyāyatīvāntariksham, dhyāyatīva dyauḥ, dhyāyantīvāpoḥ, dhyāyantīva parvatāḥ, dhyāyantīva deva-manushyāḥ* (Chhānd Up 7.6.I).

roots? Is he only his body or even his mind and intellect? His body is subject to sickness, old age and death; is death his only destiny? His mind, his proud possession, is a prisoner of its passions; its knowledge is so little and so uncertain. Is there in man some other principle of greater and surer knowledge? Is there something by knowing which all this is known or at least makes sense? Hindu spirituality sought answers to these questions; it had a vision of a higher and transformed life and its ethos was shaped by that vision.

There is nothing to show that any spokesman of prophetic religions ever raised these questions. His questions were different. They were: Who is the true God? What is His will? How can it be fulfilled? We cannot explain how, but he arrived at the conclusion, often even before he raised the question, that he knew the true God, that the Gods his neighbours knew were false, that he was the mouthpiece of this true God, and that unless others believed in him and followed him, they were damned. He felt strongly that it was his duty and God-given responsibility to propagate this view about his God and about himself. Men must be told the truth about the God and his authentic spokesman and be made to embrace this truth even by force if necessary.

The dominant ethos of prophetic religions like Christianity and Islam has been shaped by this theology. Therefore the characteristic figure of these religions is a *preacher*, a *crusader* or a *mujahid*. He has nothing to learn; he has been sent to teach and correct and wherever possible even to punish error—most men are better at preaching than at learning. He feels lost if he does not fulfil his vocation. "Woe to me if I do not preach the gospel" (1 Cor. 9.16), he says. He must go out and convert the world and conquer it for his God. The others are in darkness and he has to spread the light; he is the salt of the earth. If he is a Christian missionary, his aim, to put it in the language of an Anglican hymn, is:

> Baptize the nations; far and nigh
> The triumphs of the Cross record;
> The Name of Jesus glorify
> Till every kindred call him Lord.

This song has to go round the earth. It has to go to the east where "China's millions join the strains" and "waft them on to India's plains"; it has to go where "Islam's sway darkly broods o'er home and hearth"; it has to go to the Jews, "the long-astray," and in their "soul-blindness far-away," who were once God's own elect, but who later fell from his favour but not from his election.

As a Missionary is not taught to reflect but to act, he does not doubt that he knows the truth or whether his truths are worth knowing, or if what he knows are truths at all. He will not fail to teach, and a convert will not fail to learn, the Holy Ghost is ready at hand in both cases.

Missionary work is considered the most meritorious in Christianity. It was often accompanied by liberal use of force, but a good end justified it. St. Martin of Tours (b. AD 315) engaged in preaching to the pagans of rural Gaul while attacking their shrines with a pickaxe. Now 3675 churches and 425 villages are named after him in France alone. Pope Gregory III wrote in 739 to Boniface, the missionary who had added 100,000 souls to the Church with the help of Prince Charles, that in the day of Christ, he was "entitled to say in the presence of the saints: 'Here stand I and these children the Lord has given me. I have not lost any of them whom thou hast entrusted to me.' And again: 'It was five talents thou gave me, see how I have made profit of five talents besides.'" And then Boniface would deservedly hear the voice of God saying: "Well done, my good and faithful servant."

With this kind of understanding of man and God and its own mission, Christianity started as soon as it gathered enough strength on a long career of persecution. It persecuted pagans,[14]

[14]The Christian Emperor Theodosius ordered that a pagan shall not "venerate his lar with fire, his genius with wine, his penates with fragrant odors; he shall not burn lights to them, place incense before them, or suspend wreaths for them." He was also not to practise divination for "it is sufficient to constitute an enormous crime that any person should wish to break down the very laws of nature, to investigate forbidden matters, to disclose hidden secrets..." Some years later, even more repressive laws came and the pagan temples were completely demolished. The Theodosian

it persecuted Jews[15] from whom it was drawn, it persecuted its own heretics.[16] It persecuted cultures and peoples; it persecuted different modes of worship and different views of God. We cannot discuss here the question of how it subjugated Europe[17]

Code (Princeton) says: "We command that all their fanes, temples, and shrines, if even now any remain entire, shall be destroyed by the command of the magistrates, and shall be purified by the erection of the sign of the venerable Christian religion."

[15]Though early Christians were mostly drawn from the Jews, but the latter began to be shunned. A law came in force which laid down that "no Jew shall receive a Christian woman in marriage, nor a Christian man contract a marriage with a Jewish woman." Any such marriage was to be "considered as the equivalent of adultery." Many Jewish converts to Christianity still tended to retain old Jewish usages. This was forbidden. A law provided that any such person who "has practised circumcision, or any other Jewish rite, he shall be put to an ignominious death by the zeal and co-operation of Catholics, under the most ingenious and excruciating tortures that can be inflicted" (*lex Visigothorum*, xii, 216 (642–52).

[16]Heresy hunting is as old as Christianity itself. But as Christianity became the Imperial religion, it acquired an ominous face. Bishops sought Imperial help in crushing opposite views and the help was readily granted. Nestorius, Patriarch of Constantinople (AD 428–431), appealed to Theodosius, the fanatic Christian Emperor, in these words: "Give, O Caesar, the earth purged of heretics, and I will give you in exchange the kingdom of heaven. Exterminate with me the heretics, and with you I shall exterminate the Persians." Heresy was not only a sin, it was also a crime against the State. Christian Emperors made laws against it. By the time of Theodosius there were already 100 Statutes against it. He added more. We find in the Theodosian Code the following Edict: "It is our will that all the peoples who are ruled by the administration of our Clemency shall practise that religion which the divine Peter the Apostle transmitted to the Romans... We command that those persons who follow this rule shall embrace the name of Catholic Christians. The rest, however, whom we adjudge demented and insane, shall sustain the infamy of heretical dogmas... and they shall be smitten first by the divine vengeance and secondly by the retribution of Our own initiative..." We have merely quoted an early law which does not even remotely convey the idea of what actually happened. With time, as no pagans were left, heretics took their place and hundreds of thousands were burnt at the stake as a public celebration.

[17]Prussia and Baltic peoples were converted as late as the early thirteenth century forcibly by 'Teutonic knights' assisted by 'Sword-Brethren'. After a long and bloody struggle extending over fifty years, Prussians surrendered by 1283. According to the terms of the surrender, they were "to receive baptism within a month," and "those who declined were banished from the company of Christians, and any who relapsed were to be reduced to slavery," says Paul Johnson in his *A History of Christianity*. Lithuania was baptized a century later; she was the last to fall in Europe.

and destroyed the temples and groves of its various people,[18] how it destroyed freedom of thought, how it carried its excesses to other parts of the world, to Asia, Americas and Africa.[19] We in India know something of Islam in action, but the record of Christianity has been as black and as thorough.[20]

The world had known persecution before, but the new one was of a different species. It was theological or ideological. W.E.H. Lecky, in his *History of European Morals*, points out the difference. He says that the new persecution "has been far more sustained, systematic, and unflinching. It has been directed

[18]We have seen above how Christianity demolished pagan temples as soon as it became the State religion. It continued to do it long after. Pope Gregory the Great advised Bishop Augustine in England that "well-built" temples should not be destroyed but occupied and "transferred from the worship of idols to the service of the true God." In Northern and Central Europe, English Boniface, the so-called apostle of Germany, moved about with his retinue under the protection of the king, destroying the pagan groves and holy trees. When he was killed by angry people, he became Church's canonized saint.

[19]Benedictine monks who followed Columbus in America claimed that they destroyed 170,000 figures of religious significance to the natives in Haiti alone. Juan de Zumarraga, the first bishop of Mexico, claimed in 1531 that he had smashed over 500 temples and 20,000 idols. They were doing the same thing in Africa. A protestant missionary, writes that his dinner "was cooked with the wood of a fetish image four feet high, which was publicly hacked to pieces without a word of dissent by one of our new church members."

[20]The record of the Portuguese who occupied some coastal parts of India shows that they had nothing to learn from their Muslim counterparts. A.K. Priolkar, in his *The Goa Inquisition,* provides a list of 131 villages in the three islands of Goa, Salsete and Bardez with 601 temples, all from official sources, which were destroyed by Christians. Franciscan friars who were active in Bardez "destroyed 300 Hindu temples where false Gods were worshipped," according to a report made at that time. Jesuits were active in Salsete, and according to F. Francisco de Souza, a Jesuit historian, they destroyed at about the same time 280 temples. Dr. T.R. de Souza writes: "At least from 1540 onwards, and in the island of Goa before that year, all the Hindu idols had been annihilated...all the temples had been destroyed and their sites and building material was in most cases utilized to erect new Christian churches and chapels. Various viceregal and Church council decrees banished the Hindu priests from the Portuguese territories...Hindus were obliged to assemble periodically in Churches to listen to preaching or to the refutation of their religion" (quoted in *History of Hindu-Christian Encounters*, by Sita Ram Goel, Voice of India, New Delhi, 1989).

not merely against acts of worship, but also against speculative opinions.. It has been supported not merely as a right, but also as a duty. It has been advocated in a whole literature of theology, by classes that are specially devout, and by the most opposing sects..." Discussing further its theological sources, he says that its ethics was derived from writings in which religious massacres, on the whole the most ruthless and sanguinary on record, were said to have been directly enjoined by the Deity, in which the duty of suppressing idolatry by force was given a greater prominence than any article of the moral code, and in which the spirit of intolerance has found its most eloquent and most passionate expressions."

Lecky here speaks of Christian persecution but it holds good for Islamic one too. Islam has not only been a great imperialist, but it has also been a great suppressor of thought and opinion. It simply could not allow itself to be freely investigated and discussed by its followers. No closed ideology can. It must be accepted on faith; it must severely punish ideological 'error', 'deviation' and 'heresy'. Conformity is secured by exercising 'holy terror' (Communists call it 'revolutionary terror'). Currently the press reported of one Sadek Abdel-Kerim Malallah of Saudi Arabia, who was publicly beheaded with a single stroke of the sword for slandering God, the Quran and the prophet. He was quoted as saying that the prophet was "a liar, an impostor," and that "the religion he spread was nothing but deception" (*The Times of India*, September 5, 1992). Needless to say that this offers no deep analysis of Islam (let us however remember that this is how the unlucky victim is presented by the Interior Ministry, though he may have more to say on the subject). It takes more than an "impostor" to start a religion. In fact, one need not be an impostor in order to start or spread a religion of "deception" and, in point of fact, the founder is often quite sincere in the ordinary sense of the term and has no intention of deceiving anyone. But what if he is himself deceived? The Yoga speaks of this kind of self-deception whose source is deep in mind's opacity and duality, in *achaitanya* (unconsciousness), *vismriti* (forgetfulness), *aviveka* (lack of discernment) and *avidyā* (nescience). Not to deceive others is relatively easy, but to prevent self-deception is very much more difficult. The forces of *avidyā* are powerful; they 'in-form' and soon close in on even *sāttvika bhāvas or* good and higher thoughts and sentiments like sincerity, faith, piety and idealism and turn them to bad account. Otherwise why should a good thing like love of Al-Lāh turn into hatred of Al-Lāt and Al-'Uzzā? Why should "jealous" Gods arise at all? In Indian temples icons of gods are placed in groups on the altar as they were in Greek and other pagan temples. There was no jealousy either among the Gods or their worshippers.

There is something false about the very idea of 'founding' a religion. To say the least, it is a thoroughly materialistic idea, and it must lead to its own excesses.

Converts

The falsehood that accompanies the converting business is even worse than its intolerance. Mahatma Gandhi called proselytizing the "deadliest poison that ever sapped the foundation of truth"; and he regarded a Missionary "like any vendor of goods" though he pretends to be something else. But while a Missionary is bad enough, the convert is even worse. What Jesus said about Jewish missionaries and their converts applies to Christian missionaries and converts as well: "You traverse sea and land to make a single proselyte, you make him twice as much a child of hell as yourselves."[21] And it was from this class that the apostles first drew most of their converts.

Time has not modified Christianity's missionary aim, but only its strategy of action. The Second Vatican General Council has reiterated its old position. In its The Decree Ad Gentes on the Church's Missionary Activity, it says that the Church "is missionary by her very nature, since she draws her origin from the mission of the Son and the mission of the Holy Spirit according to the design of the Father." It again says at another place that it "must be missionary, irrespective of what God can do and

[21]Mt. 23.15

does for the salvation of those whom the Gospel does not reach." The last is a real concession, since it yields that those outside the pale of the Church are also not altogether out of the grace of God. And yet there should be no backsliding and their evangelizing should go on till the end for their own sake. Hence 700-Plans to evangelize the world. Because of the interest of the subject, we are reproducing a Review we wrote of a book of this name in *The Statesman* as an Appendix 1.

10. Ethical Code

A theology has often its own ethics. The biblical ethics is *covenantal* and it is enshrined in the Decalogue, or Ten Commandments as they are called. In the biblical history, they were spoken by Yahweh "accompanied with thunderings and lightnings and the sound of the trumpet and the mountain smoking," so much so that "people were afraid and trembled." All very impressive and dramatic, but how far they helped ethical conduct is another matter. A deepened ethics comes from a deepened view of man and not from commandments of an external agency.

We are told by Christian scholars that the Decalogue itself imitates ancient international treaties which formalized the relationship of a suzerain and a vassal. Suzerainty treaties begin with a preamble identifying the covenant lord, the speaker, and an historical prologue recounting especially the benefits previously bestowed through the favour and might of the lord. The obligations imposed on the vassal, the longest section, follow. The foremost stipulation is the requirement of loyalty to the covenant lord and negatively the proscription of all alien alliances. Another section enunciates the curses and blessings which the gods of the covenant oath would visit on the vassal in accordance with whether he transgressed or was faithful to the covenant. The biblical decalogue follows the pattern to the letter. Yahweh is the king, his chosen people his vassals who should refrain from all alien alliances.

But by the time Jesus came, the scene had changed appreciably in some ways. The 'end of the world' was expected at any time. This expectation lent a new urgency and added new element to the ethical code. We are told that Jesus's moral teaching was eschatological, that he taught interim ethics, or *interimsethik*, that is emergency legislation, or rules of conduct. These rules were to be followed till the Kingdom of Heaven came, which was expected any moment, or which was "at hand", to put it in the language of the Bible. The teaching of hating one's family (Lk.14.26) or the teaching about being eunuch (Mt. 19.10 ff) because of the imminence of the day of heaven in which there will be no marrying and giving in marriage, the teaching about having no anxiety about clothing and food (Mt. 6.25), and laying no treasures (Mt. 6.19)— they all derive from this source. The eschatological view expected the Day of Judgement soon and the speedy manifestation (*Parousia*) of Christ.

Kingdom of Heaven

The phrase occurs in the Bible at several places and at one place even as 'Kingdom of God within'. It has put many readers, particularly Hindu ones, completely off the track. They like to believe that the Bible teaches a spirituality of the Upanishads and the phrase means the ever-present reality of God within the heart.[22] But it is nothing of the sort. First, the very word 'within' is a mistranslation of the Greek word '*entos*', which means 'among' or 'in the midst'. The new Bibles including The Revised Standard Version are now giving the correct meaning.

Secondly, this interpretation does not agree with the larger biblical spirituality and tradition. In the Jewish history itself, the phrase Kingdom of God or Kingdom of Heaven came pretty late

[22]Just as they have misunderstood the phrase 'Kingdom of Heaven', many Hindus have also managed to misunderstand Jesus's words 'I and (my) Father are one'. They have built on this slender foundation a whole edifice of a biblical *advaita*. But for a truly Upanishadic *advaita*, it is not enough to say, 'I am one with the Father'; it includes the second and the third persons too and it must be able to say that 'each one is one with the Father'. At the end, it must be able to say that 'He alone is', that "That is above, That is to the west, That is to the east, That is to the south, That is to the north; That, indeed, is this whole world." *Ahaṁkārādeśa* experience is not enough; it must become *ātmādeśa* realization (Chhānd Up 7.25.1,2).

and had quite a different meaning. To begin with, it had a religious-political connotation, but by the time of Jesus it had acquired an eschatological sense, and the phrase meant 'the end of the world' or 'The Day of the Lord', which was expected any day. It becomes clear from Luke where immediately after saying "Kingdom of God is within you," he describes how soon, swiftly and unexpectedly it was to come and take people by surprise. "On that day, let him who is on the house top... not come down...; and likewise let him who is in the field not turn back...," he says (17.21–37).

Here we may quote with profit theologian H. Ridderbos on the subject. According to him, the phrase originated with the late-Jewish expectation of the future in which it denoted the decisive intervention of God, ardently expected by Israel, to restore His people's fortunes and liberate them from the power of their enemies. Later on, the national element was supplemented by the apocalyptical element. In John the Baptist's teachings, it meant the Day of divine judgement which was at hand, when God will judge and sift, and no one could evade or escape it. He, therefore, urged people to repent and baptize to prepare for the day. But in Jesus' teaching, the phrase meant he himself, that in him the great future became the 'present time'. We are also told that the phrase in its future aspect meant the history of the Church, and that today the Church is the organ of the Kingdom of Heaven.

Sermon on the Mount

No discussion of Christian ethics would be complete without mentioning a discourse called the Sermon on the Mount found in the New Testament. Like the Kingdom of Heaven, the Sermon has also caused much misunderstanding though of a different nature. It arises not from a wrong translation or a wrong interpretation but by according to the Sermon an importance it never had in the Christian tradition.

The Sermon contains lofty ethical teaching but it is not organic to the Bible. It is out of tune with much of its other moral teachings in the New Testament. It also does not agree with whatever we know of the personality of Jesus. For example, the Sermon asks us "not to judge, so that we be not judged". But Jesus is judging and condemning a good deal. He is calling whole groups of people "serpents and broods of vipers", and wondering how they would "escape being sentenced to hell"; he calls them of "evil and adulterous generation"; he even curses a fig tree for not bearing fruit probably out of the proper season (Mt. 22.18 ff). For some such and other similar reasons, some scholars believe that the Sermon derives from some non-biblical source. Some, in fact, with great cogency have shown that every sentence in the Sermon has a parallel in some contemporary source such as Egyptian Gnosticism, the Proverbs and the Talmud. They hold that the Sermon is an interpolation belonging to the period when the Bible was being assembled and was laying hands on whatever it found striking and deep in other places.[23]

The question has its importance in another context though not for our purpose here. For we are not discussing whether the Sermon is original or borrowed but how important it is in the Bible. Even as an interpolation, it has been a part of the Bible long enough and it should be regarded as such by now. But how influential and important a part it has been is another question.

It appears certain that the ethics of the Sermon belongs to a different spiritual tradition and it is out of place in a prophetic work like the New Testament. Christian scholars themselves have held that the crucial thing in the Bible is *evangelium*, the proclamation of the good news about the arrival of the Saviour. They were not even particularly conscious of the Sermon till recently when the Bible began to be debated and some people while rejecting the Saviour accepted the Bible's moral teachings. Gandhi was perhaps one of the foremost of those who made Christian theologians conscious of the Sermon. Now that they have found that it has an appeal for certain types, they have

[23]For example, it is now well-known that the story of the 'woman taken in adultery' (Jn. 8.3-11), and the passage," Father, forgive them; for they know not what they do" (Lk. 23.34) are interpolations. Earlier manuscripts do not mention them.

accepted it at least as a good device for getting a hearing in certain circles. But as the church lectionaries, writings of the Fathers and other important religious writings show, their own chief document on morals has been the Decalogue, the Ten Commandments. For example, we have before us *A Catholic Catechism*, an important teaching manual used widely for imparting knowledge of the Catholic faith; it has seventy-five pages on the Ten Commandments but only three lines on the Sermon. Various Christian churches and sects have not been much conscious of the Sermon; it is not organic to prophetic message and ethics.

So far as the common Christians are concerned, the Bible itself has come into its own only recently. For long it was a closed book for them. During most of the centuries people only knew the stories of the biblical prophets, the Saviour and Mary through their pictures in the churches, but not much more. Later on when the Bible began to be translated into vernacular languages, its reading was discouraged and even banned for quite some time. For example, the law in the British Isles was that "no woman (unless she be a noble or gentlewoman), no artificers, journeymen, servingmen, under the degree of yeoman... husbandmen or labourers, should read or use any part of the Bible under pain of fines and imprisonment."

Islam is placed more happily in this regard. It has no Sermon on the Mount or anything like it to embarrass it. Its ethics derives from its prophet, his revelations and his doings, and he intended to impose no heavy moral burdens on the believers. There are no painful contrasts between a difficult moral precept and an attractive practice. Hence there is no room for a bad conscience, no need for rationalizing and for elaborate casuistry or Jesuitry, developments so characteristic of Christianity. What ought to be done is also often pleasant and profitable to do. Islam's ethics fully accommodates a believer's mundane interests. It owes no moral obligation towards disbelieving neighbours. It is meritorious to despoil them and enslave them and their women and children.

Islam has another advantage over Christianity. There is little hiatus between its theology, ethics and law. In Christianity they tend to get mixed up as they have been also under non-Judaic influences. But Islam is of one piece. Even its law is Mosaic, not as it came through the filter of Talmud and Mishna and thus much modified and raised up, but the Mosaic law in its relative purity.[24] The following case will illustrate it. The punishment in the Old Testament for adultery is death by stoning. But by the time of Muhammad, this punishment had ceased, at least among the Jews of Medina. In a case of adultery, they had to send the two accused to Muhammad for a decision. They told their chiefs: "Go to Muhammad; if he commands you to blacken their face and award flogging them as punishment, then accept it; but if he gives verdict for stoning, then avoid it." Muhammad spared no sentiment like 'Let him who has not sinned throw the first stone', but he was grieved at people trying to soften the scripture. Allah comforted him in these words: "O Messenger, the behaviour of those who vie with one another in denying the truth should not grieve you" (Quran 5.41). The Prophet ordered the two accused to be stoned to death. Abdullah, the son of Umar the future Khalifa, reports: "I was one of those who stoned them, and I saw him (the Jew) protecting her (the Jewish lady) with his body" (*Sahih Muslim*, 4211).

11. Prophetic and Yogic Spiritualities Contrasted

Hitherto we have been discussing Judaism, Christianity and

[24]There is no intention to discount the influence of Judaic law on Christianity. Sometimes this influence was carried to ludicrous limits. For example, the Mosaic law prescribes that "when an ox gores a man or woman, the ox shall be stoned." We have many cases of court trials of 'criminal' animals in medieval Europe. We may cite one quoted by G.G.Coulton in his *Life in the Middle Ages*: A young pig on a farm mutilated a young child of its owner. After a trial the court decided: "Wherefore we make known that we, in detestation and horror of this case aforesaid, and in order to keep exemplary justice, have bidden, judged, sentenced, pronounced and appointed that the said hog, being now bound in prison under lock and key in the Abbey aforesaid, shall by the common hangman be hanged by the neck until he be dead upon a wooden gibbet..." In another case in Bale, in 1474, a cock was condemned to be burnt alive for having laid an egg, in derogation of its proper sex.

Islam. They have their differences which in some ways are important. For example, the Jews have not claimed a world mission and except rarely their faith has been only for themselves and for those who cared to join them. True, they have believed that the truths of their faith are universal, but they have not claimed that these truths are exclusive to their faith. Bernard Lewis tells us of a Talmudic dictum that the righteous of all faiths have their place in paradise. It is different from Christianity and Islam where each claims to be the sole custodian of God's final revelation to mankind and neither admits salvation outside its own creed.[25]

However, they have powerful similarities which make them belong to one species or family, the family of prophetic religions. They share important common traits which mark them off from yogic spiritualities like Hinduism. The two differ radically in their approach and ethos on most important questions relating to man, divinity, nature, ethics, salvation. Here we shall briefly mention a few points.

Hinduism approaches the problem from various angles, one very important angle being man himself and his consciousness with which he is most familiar. It begins by asking the question: What is man? And it introduces us progressively to his deeper facets. It finds that man is more than what he appears to be, that his roots are deep. Taittirīya Upanishad, for example, tells us that man is made up of various sheaths, each more subtle than the preceding one. It tells us that behind his more external personality made up of the physical, psychic and mental parts, there is another, a more intimate one; it is of the form of knowl-

[25]Dante places even Socrates, Plato, Thales, Zeno, Seneca, Euclid, Galen and so on in the Limbo, the first circle of Hell. Why? Because though "they sinned not; and though they have merit, it suffices not: for they had not Baptism, which is the portal of the faith...and seeing they were before Christianity, they worshipped not God aright." He even placed Adam, Noah, Abraham and Moses there, but a "Mighty One, crowned with sign of victory (Jesus) came and took them away" *vide 1 Peter 3* (Divine Comedy, Canto IV).

Similarly, Muhammad too had no place even for the best of non-Muslims in his Paradise and he sent even his parents and kindly uncle to hell.

edgẹ (*vijñāna-maya*), and it is made up of faith, the right, the true, yoga, and the vast (*śraddhā, rita, satya, yoga, mahas*). Behind this, in turn, stands another self called *ānanda-maya*, which consists of delight and bliss, from which we all come and into which we all return.

Man's normal consciousness is obscure; its knowledge is uncertain and it is hardly an instrument of truth. But as man goes deeper into himself, he meets another consciousness which is luminous, self-aware, and in touch with all. The Upanishads speak of a consciousness which is unified (*ekībhūta*), massed knowledge (*prajñāna-ghana*), consisting of joy (*ānanda-maya*); it feeds on bliss (*ānanda-bhuj*), light is its mouth (*chetomukha*), and it knows all (*prājña*).

In prophetic scriptures, we do not find any such thing. In fact, even the word consciousness in this deeper sense is not there. Perhaps the prophetic religions were more concerned with the other question, What is God? However, there is nothing to show that they ever raised this question, though we have their answer without knowing how they arrived at it. As soon as they knew their god, they decided that he was the true one and the gods of Canaanites, Hittites, Hivites were false; that Jehovah alone was true and that Baal, Ashtoreth, Chomesh, Molech and, later on, Apollo and Jupiter were false. Similarly, they found that Al-Lāh alone was true and Al-Lāt, Al-'Uzzā, Al-Manāt and the Gods of their neighbours were false.

Hinduism raised questions about God as it did about man, and the result was a great spiritual deepening and enrichment. Hinduism gave us Gods that were friends of men and of each other;[26] it gave us Gods that were conceived as mothers, fathers, consorts, sons and daughters; it gave us Gods that were one and

[26]In Hindu conceptualizing, Gods are friends; one God reflects all others and all reflect the Supreme. "He is Brahmā, He is Vishṇu, He is Rudra, Prajāpati, Agni, Varuṇa, Vāyu, Indra, Moon, Yama, Earth, He is All," according to Maitri Upanishad. Similarly, the Egyptian God 'Ra' is identified with seventy-five other Gods in the famous "Litany of Ra". According to Aeschylus, the Greek God Zeus is "the air, the earth, the sky. He is all things and is higher than all this." In none of these there is a tradition of a "jealous God".

many, immanent as well as transcendent at the same time; it gave us Gods of various *dhyānas* (Buddha spoke of Gods of the first, second, third, fourth *dhyānas*); it gave us Gods of *samprajñāta* and *asamprajñāta samādhis*. It has One Thousand Names (*sahasranāma*) of Vishṇu, of Śiva, of Śri Lakshmī, of Gāyatrī, of Ganeśa, of Lalitā. There is nothing like it in prophetic religions. Christianity lacks 'Names of God' altogether — it has much christology but little worthwhile theology. Islam through Sufism (itself an import) has imbibed a tradition of 'Ninety-nine Names of Allah', but the tradition fails to articulate Names of deeper spirituality— here we particularly mean names relating to higher states of *samādhi* and *prajñā*. We however cannot go into this question here but shall merely state that there cannot be a developed knowledge of Gods without a developed knowledge of Self. *Atma-jñāna* and *Deva-jñāna* go together.

Prophetic religions conceive their god differently. They all believe that there is a special God who has a special people, and who is known through a special intermediary. They are all agreed on the special God, though they disagree on the special people and the special intermediary. They also believe that this God's self-revelation is a one-time event which takes place through a chosen intermediary—a one-time man becoming an all-time man. According to Christianity, it took place in Jesus, and according to Islam it culminated and also ended in Muhammad.

The God of this species of spirituality also gave us a special moral code, a theological morality. The common morality says, Be kind to your fellow men to please your God. But the new moral code says that you will earn more merit in the sight of your God if you are harsh towards the unbelievers and even kill them. According to the older code people rob and kill because they are bad; in the new code, they are required to kill and rob because they are pious and good. In fact, the sinners of Christianity and Islam have often been better than their saints and pious leaders. If these so-called saints knew as much about themselves as they claim to know about their God, they should stay away from a good deal they do.

Dharma

Hinduism has nothing like this code; we also find in it highest thinking on ethics. It has a concept peculiar to it—the concept of *dharma*. It is difficult to define or even explain it. Its older Vedic name was *rita*. The concept is both ethical as well as metaphysical. It says that man ought to do what is right and good, but it adds that to do the right is also man's very nature, the law of his true being. He is being himself by doing what is right and good.

It follows that we should be good, but to be good all of us have not to do the same thing and all cannot be good in the same way. We differ in our talents and in our opportunities. A soldier does good in a different way than a civilian. Householders and those who have the means do good by doing charitable acts, by digging wells and building hospitals and temples—activities called *pūrta* in Hindu Shastras; others by a charitable disposition. Sanyāsins do good through goodwill and prayer, and by cultivating equanimity, compassion, and renunciation.

It is obvious that in this approach, *dharma* cannot be a fixed command. One's *dharma* cannot be greater than one's being and knowledge. A man grows in *dharma* as he grows in his being and knowledge. The aim of Hindu teaching is therefore to help a man to grow in *sattva*, in his inner being, in his mind and soul, and a great ethical life, the life of *śīla*, is its natural concomitant.

Ethics in this approach cannot be one monolithic code. Here it allows plurality, different paths, different ways. Here one serves the Great Good by serving according to one's psychic and intellectual endowment, talent, capacity, opportunity, and circumstances. Indian ethic allows plurality of duties and vocations. Bhishma of the Mahabharata "salutes Him whose very Self is *dharma*, but whom followers of diverse paths in the pursuit of diverse ends serve in diverse ways".[27]

Prophetic religions also deny any direct God-man relation-

[27]*yam prithag-dharmācharnāh prithag-dharma-phalaishṇah prithag-dharmaih saṁcharanti tasmai dharmātmane namah*

ship. There is no possibility nor probably any need for a direct contact for oneself with God. This was done long ago for us all by someone else, and the best we can do is to follow him and join the party inaugurated by him, his holy church or *ummah*. They teach a surrogate spirituality.

But a predominantly yogic spirituality rejects these premises. It preaches a higher life accessible to all, that is all who fulfil its conditions; it believes in higher celestial beings; it believes in God and Gods, and that they can be seen and experienced and one can live in fellowship with them, and it can be done by all who approach them in devotion, sincerity and truth; it believes that the unfoldment of higher life is not an arbitrary process or a chance happening but that it is a lawful process, and that all who work for it have a share in it; that in fact this life is a man's own innermost life and truth, and that he knows Gods when he is most God-like.

It is obvious therefore that in this kind of spirituality, there can be no place for a one-man revelation. In any case, such a revelation is no good for others. A truth must become your own if it is to do good to you. One cannot live another man's truth.

Most advanced spiritualities in the world have held this approach. Today, their most prominent living representative is Hinduism or the *Sanātana Dharma* with its family of religions.

12. Mystical Tradition

These basic differences arise from the fact that Hindu spirituality is deeply introspective. It has developed a great discipline of inward looking which is called Yoga. At some stage, Christianity and Islam too had borrowed certain elements from this source but these could not fit into their system of belief. So these were soon either banished or treated peripherally. The elements that survived were subordinated to prophetic ideologies. Today, mystical theology in Christianity and Sufism in Islam have no independent role; they are mere handmaids of their hosts. The subject falls outside the scope of the discussion here, but we shall still make a brief reference.

Some mysticism was literally smuggled into Christianity

near about AD 500. One Bar Sudali, a Syrian monk familiar with Vedantic thought (most Western writers like to call it neo-Platonism), as it appears from his book, wrote on the subject of higher mysticism under the ghost-name of Dionysius the Areopagite, converted to Christianity by Paul in the first century. This cover name proved useful and the writings of Pseudo-Dionysius, as Sudali came to be known to posterities, gained some acceptability and honour though not much use in certain Christian circles. His writings influenced Scotus Erigena, an Irish who taught at the court of Charles the Fat in the ninth century. Through his writings, the thought of Dionysius became known to several countries of Western Europe. In the fourteenth century, we meet Rhineland mystics powerfully influenced by this current, Eckhart being the most celebrated name among them. In their approach, there was no particular place for the God of monotheists ("you prattle too much about God," Eckhart said) and the Son of Christian persuasion; therefore these mystics were often anathematized.

In its long history, Christianity had little place for the method of self-reflection in its spiritual praxis. Its hermits and more pious monks practised fasting, vigils, and extreme and sometimes even competitive self-mortification. The lives of Christian saints are full of accounts of their "temptations" (for example, St. Anthony's have become a legend), their frequent encounters with the Devil and how they worsted him. Saint Gothlac often engaged in hand-to-hand combats with demons. Saint Dunstan pulled the Devil's nose with a pair of red-hot tongs. Luther threw an ink-pot at him. St. Dominic, as he began discoursing to the sisters of a convent on the subject of the Devil, found that "the enemy of mankind came on the scene in the shape of a sparrow." Of course, he was caught, and after plucking his feathers one by one, Dominic allowed him to go saying: "Fly now if you can, O enemy of mankind." Such were the victories scored over the enemy of God and man. In all this there was little place for contemplative methods.

In Islam too, mysticism in the shape of Sufism is more of a graft than a natural flowering. Rabia who belongs to the second century of Islam really represents an old pagan-Arab tradition. Al-Hallaj and Abu Yazid Bistami who belong to the third century of the Islamic era represent mainly Hindu-Buddhist tradition. Abu Yazid's grandfather was a Zoroastrian and his teacher was Abu Ali of Sindh. According to the *Dictionary of Islam*, Sufism "is but a Muslim adaptation of the Vedanta school of Hindu philosophers."

Prophetic Islam would have died from its own formalism and legalism, but Sufism saved it from this fate by importing into it some principle of warmth and internality. But in this association, it itself suffered a great setback. In fact, higher mysticism was incompatible with prophetic Islam and it disappeared soon enough. The Sufism that survived and even prospered was tame and promised to subserve prophetism. Some great Sufi poets like Rumi and Attar convey a wrong impression of Islamic Sufism in general; they have been its show-pieces, not its representative figures. Mainstream Sufism has been represented by its *silsilās* like the Naqshbandiyya, Qadiriyya, Chishtiyya, Dervish, Marabout, Ribat, etc. They had no independent ideology of their own and they only served the spiritual-intellectual categories (*manīshā*) of prophetic Islam; in fact, they became its most willing spokesmen. They never questioned its dogmas, not even its barbaric ideas about the *kafirs*, the *jihād*, the *zimmīs*, the *dār al-harb*. There is nothing to show that they ever spoke against Islamic wars and oppression. On the other hand, as their history shows they were part and parcel of Islamic Imperialism, its enthusiastic sappers and miners and also its beneficiaries. According to the *Encyclopaedia Britannica*, the Dervish and Sufis have fought against the unbelievers in time of war. The devotees have accompanied the Shaikh or Murshid or Pīr to the threatened frontiers. Thus the *murabit*, "one who pickets on a hostile frontier," has become the *marabout* or *dervish* of Algeria. Similarly, *riba* means a 'frontier fort', or a 'fortress for the defence of Islam'; *ribat* also came to mean a monastery and a religious-military community which performed garrison duty at the frontiers of *dār al-Islām* and waged holy wars against its neighbours. The *al-murabitun* played a great role in the Moorish annexation of Spain. In India, the sufis have been an important limb of Islamic Imperialism and expansion. The spiritual dimension was for them only a secondary concern.

The Inward Journey

In the language of the Kaṭhopanishad, most men look outward, but some seeking a higher law and life turn their gaze inward and behold the soul face to face. They become aware of a larger, secret life buried within. They realize that through earnest endeavour and devout invocation, this life can be uncovered and made dynamic and manifest in their lives.

For undertaking this inward journey, the soul has all the provisions in its possession. But different seekers are differently endowed, and each has to make the best use of his own special endowment. Hinduism in its long career has developed several methods; some emphasize the importance of devotion, some of unflinching effort, some of knowledge and discrimination. Indian sages have also chosen different symbols and aspects and Names. Some have emphasized a personal God, some the impersonal Brahma. Some have given us positive definitions while others have described negatively what they sought and saw. But though apparently different they all have a common centre; they all insist on the need for shedding lower life in order to find and unite with higher life; they all emphasize the need of Yoga, which among other things includes one-pointedness, concentrated attention, devotion, progressive purification of the inner being, and discrimination.

As a seeker advances on this path, he becomes increasingly aware of his higher nature. He finds that fearlessness, purification of the inner being, steadfastness in Yoga, self-restraint and worship, study of the Shastras, austerity and harmlessness, truthfulness, compassion for all living beings, forgiveness, fortitude, purity, absence of guile, crookedness, fickleness, envy and pride, mildness, modesty, peace, renunciation, and uncovetousness, etc., are great realities, great truths of the spirit, great divine properties (*daivī sampad*). Unless one is born in and to them, there is no true spiritual birth. One should learn to cherish them and make them his own.

The seeker becomes aware of the larger God-life that surrounds him, and of his "heavenly roots" from which he derives his sustenance. He discovers that what sustains him also sustains the world, that truthfulness, loftiness, power, consecration, austerity, the knowledge of the Supreme, and worship uphold the earth[28] as well. He realizes that mere hedonism and consumerism are self-defeating and cannot stand alone and survive; that even our more secular satisfactions require a life of *dharma* to sustain them, and that *dharma* itself is rooted in *moksha*, in dispassion, renunciation and equal-mindedness.

He becomes aware of great liberating forces, the forces of spiritual faith, effort, mindfulness, *samādhi* and wisdom. But he also becomes aware of forces that bind him to a lower life, the forces of desire, aversion, infatuation, ego, and nescience (*rāga, dvesha, abhiniveśa, asmitā, avidyā*)— or *kleśas* as they are called — that feed his phenomenal life; he finds his eyes, his ears, his nose, in fact his whole being on fire, burning in the fire of desire, of anger, of hankering, of false ego and infatuation; he becomes aware how they fabricate a false life, and how a man moves from one birth to another caught in their web, how though the man dies physically, these forces abide in some subtle condition as pre-dispositions, as *saṁskāras*, shaping a new life for him. He realizes that the law of *karma* is difficult to transgress; that though a man may have celestial visions and voices, but these forces have a seed power and having remained dormant for a long time come to life again in their own time; that it needs much grace and spiritual wisdom before they are conquered.

Yoga gives not only Self-knowledge, *ātma-jñāna*, it also gives knowledge of God or Gods. The man on the inner journey not only realizes that God or Gods are within him, but he also realizes that he is within them. On this path, one meets many divine figures which are also truths of his own soul. Here, there

[28]*satyam brihad-ritam-ugram dīkshā tapo brahma yajñah prithivīm dhārayanti* (Ath Veda 12.1.1).

is no God who hates 'other' Gods; for there are no 'others' here. In a yogic God there is no hatred and no otherness of certain non-yogic Gods. He is in all the Gods and all other Gods are in him; he has also no reason to detest partners, for he does not become less for having them, nor does he cease to be Himself on that account. He realizes *advaita*; he realizes that God alone is, which is quite a different thing from saying that there is only one God; he realizes that 'God alone' is not the same thing as a lone God.

Here one is united with all humanity and there are no infidels and heathens here. In fact, here all walls fall and the seeker feels one with all living beings, past and present and future, on this or other planes. He also feels one with elements; the sky, the sun, night and day, the four directions, the wind, the fire, the waters and the earth— all are kins and friends. All have a place and all are part of a cosmic holiness and goodness.[29] Needless to say that this deepened vision also gives a lofty ethics.

Here one also becomes aware of "the Unknown God"; one realizes that 'unknowability' or 'unknownness' is God's great attribute. Therefore, the attempt of those like Paul who pretend to declare Him[30] is laughable. He is not known by those who say they know him, but he is known by those who say they know him not.

One becomes aware of the true sources of the Shastras like the Upanishads, the Gita, the Pitakas, the Mahabharata and the Ramayana. Their source is a deeper seeing, a deeper compassion, a deeper intuition of unity and transcendence. They come from those established in a consciousness deep like the ocean.

[29]Prophetic scriptures show no particular consciousness of elements like the sky, the wind, the fire, the waters, the earth. They are no more than *creatures* meant for man's use and exploitation. But the Upanishads use them for spiritual contemplation and find them great vehicles of the Spirit and see behind them divinity. In Buddhist Yoga, they are often used as *karma-sthānas* or *kasiṇs*, objects of *dhyāna*. Prophetic scriptures show no great consciousness of humanity or man either. They know man mostly under the figure of a heathen, an unbeliever or an infidel.

[30]Acts 17.22 ff.

They are not effusions of a temporary enthusiasm.[31]

13. Non-Yogic *Samādhis*

All these experiences and insights belong to the yogic development and are the fruits of yogic *samādhi* and yogic *prajñā*. There is also however an opposite development and the yogic literature also hints at non-yogic *samādhis*.

Unfortunately, traditional commentators on the *Pātañjala Yogadarśana* did not develop this hint and concentrated on expounding only the yogic *samādhi*. *Viśuddhi Mārga*, the great Buddhist treatise on Yoga, does the same. After observing that *samādhi* is of many kinds but discussing them all would cause distraction, it limits itself to the elucidation of the *samādhi* of the *kuśala-chitta*, or purified mind.

Vyasa, the great commentator of *Yogadarśana*, does somewhat better. He tells us that mind has five habitual states or planes (*bhūmis*): *mūḍha* (dull or inert), *kshipta* (restless, or probably it is *saṁkshipta* and means contracted), *vikshipta* (scattered), *ekāgra* (one-pointed), and *niruddha* (stopped). He makes a further pregnant statement that *samādhi* is natural to mind and it can take place on all *bhūmis* (*sārvabhauma*); but he adds a warning that the *samādhis* of the first three *bhūmis* are non-yogic and only the *samādhis* of the last two *bhūmis* are

[31]If you look at prophetic scriptures, you don't find higher spiritual truths there though they may have other merits. The Bible, for example, is a contribution to literature. It is eminently readable and quotable and in spite of much ferocity and cruelty in many places, it has passages of great beauty and power. Some of the deepest emotions of the vital man— his enmities, hatreds, revenge, sorrow, defeat, piety etc.— find eloquent expressions there. Those who have this kind of book can truly claim to possess a great literature.

As regards the Quran, it is a contribution to literature neither. And though it is the effusion of one man, it is highly disjointed and becomes intelligible only with the help of commentaries.

The most objectionable thing about the two books however is not that they lack higher spirituality, but that they teach and practise theological ethics, the worst of its kind. Many peoples have practised ordinary humanist ethics without ever having heard of *advaita;* they have instinctively treated others as if they were themselves. Theological code taught by prophetic scriptures however overpowered humanist ethics.

yogic. Only the yogic *samādhi* leads to spiritual development.

This subject could be further discussed with great advantage. But the succeeding commentators neglected further elucidation. This self-limitation is good for the purpose in hand, but it has a serious disadvantage too. Considering that the two kinds of *samādhis* are not unoften confused with each other, it would have served the cause of clarity if both were discussed and their differences pointed out. After all, the Gita does it; in its last two chapters, it discusses various spiritual truths like austerity, faith, duty, knowledge in their triple expressions and sharply distinguishes their *sāttvika* forms from their *rājasika* and *tāmasika* imitations. The same could be said of *samādhis* and their pure and impure forms distinguished.

The elucidation of non-yogic *samādhis* or ecstasies has also its positive value and peculiar concern. It could help to explain quasi-religious phenomena which, sadly, have been only too numerous and too important in the religious history of man. Many creeds seemingly religious sail under false labels and spread confusion. As products of a fitful mind, they could but make only a temporary impression and their life could not but be brief. But as projections of a mind in some kind of *samādhi*, they acquire unusual intensity, a strength of conviction and tenacity of purpose (*mūdhāgraha*) which they could not otherwise have.

The message is clear. Developing Vyasa's hint, we may say that even the lower *bhūmis* (*kāma-bhūmis*) have their characteristic *samādhis*, trances or their own Revelations, their own Prophets and their own Deities. They project ego-gods and desire-gods and give birth to *dvesha-dharmas* and *moha-dharmas*, hate-religions and delusive ideologies. All these projections have qualities very different from the qualities of the projections of the yogic *bhūmi*.

14. Gods of Non-Yogic *Bhūmis*

For example, the god of the *yoga-bhūmi* of *Pātañjala Yoga* is free, actually and potentially, from all limiting qualities like desire, aversion, hankering, ego and nescience; free from all actions, their consequences, present or future, active or latent. Or in the language of *Pātañjala Yoga*, he is untouched by *kleśa-karma-vipāka-āśaya*. But the god of the ecstasies of non-yogic *bhūmi* or *kāma-bhūmi* is very different. He has strong likes and dislikes and has cruel preferences. He has his favourite people, churches and *ummahs*, and his implacable enemies. He is also very egoistic and self-regarding; he can brook no other god or gods. He insists that all gods other than himself are false and should not be worshipped. He is a "jealous god", as he describes himself in the Bible. And he "whose name is Jealous" is also full of "fierce anger" (*aph*). He commands his chosen people that when he brings them to the promised land and delivers its people into their hands, "Thou shalt smite them, and utterly destroy them; thou shalt make no covenant with them, nor show mercy unto them...thou shall destroy their altars, and break down their images, and cut down their groves... For thou art an holy people unto the Lord...."[32] He promises to his people: "I will be an enemy to your enemies and an adversary to your adversarie"; and they return the sentiment: "Do I not hate them , O Lord, that hate thee? Yea, I hate them with perfect hatred."[33]

The Allah of the Quran exhibits about the same qualities. He is god of wrath (*ghazab*); on those who do not believe in him and his prophets, he wreaks a terrible punishment (*azāb al-azīm*). In the same vein, he is also a mighty avenger (*azīzu'l intiqām*). He is also a god of "plenteous spoils" (*maghnīm kasīrat*). He tells the believers how he repulsed their opponents and caused them to inherit the land, the houses and the wealth of the disbelievers, and the land they had not trodden.[34] He follows the spirit of Jehovah who promised his chosen people that he would give them "great and goodly cities they builded not, and wells which they digged not, vineyards and olive trees they planted not" (Deut. 6.10-11).

Allah is merciful too but his mercy extends to the believers only. According to a *hadis*, the prophet said that there "would be

[32]Deut. 7.1-6.
[33]Exod. 23.22, and Ps. 139.22,23.
[34]Quran 33.27.

people among the Muslims with as heavy sins as a mountain, but Allah would forgive them and he would place in their stead the Jews and the Christians." In fact, on "the Day of Resurrection Allah would deliver to every Muslim a Jew or a Christian and say: That is your rescue from Hell-Fire."[35]

No wonder this kind of god inspired serious doubts and questions among thinking people. Philo and Origen had to do a lot of allegorizing to make him acceptable. Some early Christian Gnostics simply rejected him. They said that he was an imperfect being presiding over an imperfect moral order; some even went further and regarded him as the principle of Evil. Some Gnostic thinkers called him "Samael", a blind God or the God of the blind; others called him "Ialdabaoth", the son of Chaos.

He continues to offend the moral sense of our rational age too. Thomas Jefferson thinks that the "Bible God is a being of terrific character, cruel, vindictive, capricious and unjust." Lincoln wrote a pamphlet against Christianity itself. But both being publicmen had to cover their tracks. Thomas Paine says of the Bible that "it would be more consistent that we call it the work of a demon than the word of God."

Hindus have done a lot of thinking on the subject of ecstasy and *samādhi,* yet they regard it with utmost superstition. They fail to see that any agitated state of mind is not *samādhi* and any trance utterance or vision is not a *samādhi* utterance or vision. They will buy any outrage if it is sold under a religious label or in the name of a god, saints, or prophets. They have also a great weakness for what they describe as "synthesis." In that name, they will lump together most discordant things without any sense of their propriety and congruity, intellectual or spiritual. However, a few names like Bankim Chandra, Swami Dayananda, Vivekananda, Aurobindo and Gandhi are exceptions to the rule. Bankim finds the god of the Bible "a despot"; and he thinks that Jesus's doctrine of "eternal punishment" in the "everlasting Fire" is "devilish." Swami Dayananda remembers how the biblical "Lord sent a pestilence... and there fell seventy

[35]*Sahih Muslim,* 6665–6669.

thousand men of Israel,"[36] his own Chosen People, and it puts him off. He observes that even "the favours of a capricious god like him so quick in his pleasure are full of danger," as the Jews know it only too well. The Swami further argues in his usual unsparing way that the Allah and Shaitān of the Quran, according to its own showing, are alike.

Psychic Source

But to reject is not to explain. Why should a god have to have such qualities? And why should a being who has such qualities be called God? And why should he have so much hold? Yoga provides an answer. It says that though not a truly spiritual being, he is thrown up by a deeper source in the mind. He is some sort of a psychic formation and carries the strength and attraction of such a formation; he also derives his qualities and dynamism from the *chitta-bhūmi* in which he originates.

This will explain that the biblical God is not unique and he is not a historical oddity. He has his source in man's psyche and he derives his validity and power from there; therefore he comes up again and again and is found in cultures widely separated. This god has his own ancestry, his own sources from which he is fed, his own tradition and principle of continuity, self-renewal and self-validation.

Not many people know that a similar God, Il Tengiri, presided also over the life of Chingiz Khan and bestowed Revelations on him. Minhājus Sirāj, the mid-thirteenth century historian, tells us in his *Tabqāt-i-Nāsiri,* that "after every few days, he (Chingiz Khan) would have a fit and during his unconsciousness he would say all sorts of things... Some one would write down all he said, put (the papers) in a bag and seal them. When Chingiz recovered consciousness, everything was read out to him and he acted accordingly. Generally, in fact always, his designs were successful."

In this, one can see unmistakable resemblance with the revelations or *waḥy* of the prophetic tradition.

[36] I Chr. 21.14

15. Intrusions and Eruptions

In actual life, one seldom meets truths of the *kāma-bhūmi* and *krodha-bhūmi* unalloyed. Often they are mixtures and touched by intrusions from the truths of the *yoga-bhūmi* above. This however makes them still more virulent; it puts a religious rationalization on them. It degrades the higher without uplifting the lower. The theories of *jihād*, crusade, conversion and *da'wa* become spiritual tasks, Commandments of God, religious obligations, vocations and duties of a Chosen People. "See my zeal for the Lord," says Jehu, an army captain anointed as king at the command of Jehovah. Bound to follow His will, he called all the prophets, servants, priests and worshippers of Baal on the pretext of organizing Baal's service and when they were gathered, his guards and captains "smote them with the edge of the sword," and "they demolished the image of Baal, and demolished the house of Baal, and made it a draught house [latrine] unto this day" (2 Kings 10.25, 27).

Lower impulses are indeed difficult to conquer; they seem to have an autonomous life of their own. Even those who have experienced the truths of higher life are subject to their pull, and eruptions from below are common enough in their lives too. Hence the insistence of Yoga on a moral and spiritual discipline and on inner purification. In fact, the whole of Yoga could be summed up in one word: purification or *chitta-prasāda* or *chitta-śuddhi*. Indeed it knows that without purification, even Yoga could be put to a negative use. In fact, it is done in "Spiritual Exercises" of the Jesuits, which has adopted the initial limbs of Yoga but which uses them not for liberation, but for the intensification of certain fond ideas and beliefs, for theological self-conditioning.

Therefore the Yoga insists that the aspirant should first be established in *śīla*, *yama* and *niyama*, self-restraint, harmlessness and truthfulness. Yoga cares only for such *samādhi* as is built on the foundation of a developed ethical life. Next it insists on the progressive purification of *samādhi* itself through the purification of *antah-karaṇa*, *manas* and *buddhi*, of *smriti* and *dhyāna*. The mind should expand by constantly dwelling on benevolence, compassion, sympathetic joy and equanimity (*maitrī, karuṇā, muditā,* and *upekshā*).

16. Purification of *Samādhi*

As we have learnt to distinguish the yogic *samādhi* from the non-yogic one, we should also remember that even yogic *samādhi* is not something fixed and given once for all. Yogic *samādhi* itself needs progressive purification; it has many grades and stations and each grade has its characteristic qualities. If the mind is sufficiently purified, it automatically moves from one stage to the next and deeper one, which is different both in what it contemplates and in the qualities of that contemplation. Each stage has its characteristic quality, flavour or *rasa.*

The subject is big and we shall do here with the briefest reference. *Viśuddhi Mārga* describes this movement very clearly. It divides the movement into several *dhyānas* and *samāpattis*. It tells us that the first four or five (depending on one's enumeration) *dhyānas* are characterized by *vitarka* (reflection), *vichāra* (sustained application), *prīti* (joy), *sukha* (felicity), *ekāgratā* (one pointedness), and *smriti* (mindfulness) in the ascending order of yogic subtleness. In the fourth *dhyāna*, the coarse limbs of the earlier *dhyānas* leave or are rather in abeyance, yielding place only to "mindfulness purified by *upekshā*", or equal-mindedness or *samatā* of the Gita. This equal-mindedness opens the door to many kinds of infinities and universalities (*ānantyas*). Beyond these infinities lies the *nirodhabhūmi* of *Pātañjala Yoga* or the *nirvāṇa-bhūmi* of the Buddhists.

For our purpose, we need not go into this larger Yoga at all. It will suffice to point out that the higher Indian spirituality begins with the fourth *dhyāna* which is characterized by equal-mindedness. On the other hand, much of what we find in the scriptures of prophetic religions does not emanate from the yogic *bhūmi*, but in portions which do touch this plane, the truths are restricted to the first two or three *dhyānas*. For example, the New Testament on several occasions and at many places emphasizes the importance of faith, piety, zest, zeal, belief, joy, promise, confidence and fervour—all truths of the first *dhyānas*. But even in these places, we find no mention of *samatā*, equal-mindedness, the base of further truths like universal sympathy (*jīva-dayā*), the great law of *dharma* upholding all, self-emptying, *nirvāṇa* or *moksha*, or liberation, *ātma-jñāna*, and *advaita*—the staples of Indian spirituality.

Though no effort is lost on the path of Yoga as the Gita teaches, there is however always a danger of relapse unless the higher vision (*prajñā*) opens up. The *śrottāpanna* is not the same as an *anāgāmī*; a seeker must either go up or he will go down. The truths of the initial *dhyānas* are not secure unless they are fortified by a higher vision. But in the biblical case we are discussing, these truths had no support from a higher *prajñā*; on the other hand, they were under the gravitational pull of a different kind of vision, the vision that derived from monolatry and prophetism. No wonder that the Church lost those truths so soon and they turned into their own caricatures. Almost from the beginning, the Church's zeal turned into zealotry and became persecutory, its faith became narrow and dogmatic, its confidence arrogant and sectarian. In India's spiritual tradition, a faulty vision (*prajñā-aparādha*) is considered a great poisoner.

Thus in the absence of a true science of interiority, Christianity took to an ideology of physical and outward expansion. It holds good for Islam too. They both have faced an inner problem — the problem of an undeveloped spirituality. This has constituted danger to the rest of the humanity as well.

17. Conclusion

Gore Vidal says that from a "barbaric Bronze Age text known as Old Testament, three anti-human religions have evolved — Judaism, Christianity and Islam"; he also calls them "sky-god religions." There would have been no harm if they had a yogic sky-god, for a yogic god is in all the gods and includes all other gods—gods of the earth as well as of the heaven and beyond. Moreover, as man is kin both to the earth as well as to the sky, he has to have gods of both and also of all that is beyond. But the trouble is that the prophetic god is not a yogic god; in fact, he is hardly a spiritual being; he is a fanatic entity, an intolerant and hegemonic idea.

The sky-godders have been great persecutors. The world has been under their attack, both physical and ideological, for a long time. India has known their attacks for a thousand years. This has inflicted on the country not only great political and economic damage, but has also put it under great psychological and ideological strain. Hindus have become apologetic about their most cherished ideas. Monolatrous ideologies have come to enjoy great prestige, the prestige that comes from having been in power for so long.

During the days of Islamic and Christian rule, Hindus tried to cope with the situation in several ways. First, they tried to 'reform' themselves and be like their rulers; they claimed that Hinduism had already all the 'virtues' of Christianity and Islam — one God, a revealed Book, and prophets. This spirit infected all, even non-Hindu sects. For example, when the Parsis were told in 1860s by Martin Haug, a German scholar, that true Zoroastrianism was monotheistic and had no idol worship and no rituals, they were very much relieved. The Brahmo Samaj, the Arya Samaj, and the Akalis also claimed monotheism and iconoclasm. Some monks of the Ramakrishna Mission have also learnt to think that they do their Guru more honour by treating him as the founder of a religion like Moses, Jesus and Mohammad, than as a *rishi*, a confirmer and carrier of an ancient spiritual tradition. In the case of the Akalis, the new look has also become the basis of a new separatist-militant politics. In all this work of self-introspection and self-reform, no need was felt of giving a closer look to the religions of the rulers as well. The ideology of an exclusive god making himself known through an exclusive person, a special apostle, and an exclusive revelation remained unquestioned.

The second way the Hindus adopted was that of "synthesis". The synthesizers claimed that all religions preach the same thing. They found in the Bible and the Quran all the truths of the Upanishads and vice versa. They culled passages from various scriptures to prove their point. That they found little in the

Quran or the Bible[37] in that line did not dampen their spirit. They secured their point by taking recourse to selective quotes, by picking on stray phrases, by giving them a meaning which they did not have. They misrepresented the spirit of different preachings by slurring over important differences and by making too much of incidental agreements. Some took to allegorizing and read deep esoteric meanings[38] in passages which plainly told a different story. It is by such methods that they proved that the Bible and the Quran were no different from the Upanishads. Thus they became propagators of Christianity and Islam among their own people.

Besides the rationalists, many seekers in the West had learnt to reject Christianity as an inadequate spiritual ideology. But under the auspices of Hindu synthesizers, it began to find a new acceptance. Today some of the best propagandists of Christianity and Islam are Hindu synthesizers.

Struggle for Cultural Freedom

The long period under the two Imperialisms, Islamic and Christian, has ended, but they have left a powerful legacy behind. India became politically free in 1947, but it is ruled by anti-Hindu Hindus. The old mental slavery continues and it has yet to win its cultural and intellectual independence.

India is entering into the second phase of its freedom struggle: the struggle for regaining its Hindu identity. The new struggle is as difficult as the old one. Hindus are disorganized,

[37]Aldous Huxley, in his *The Perennial Philosophy* consisting of extensive quotes from various religious literature (about 40 percent of the book is quotes), could not find a single quote from the Quran, nor any direct quote from the four Gospels in support of the thesis of a common mystical ground shared by all religions.

[38]Hindus are good at this game of self-deception. For example, one bright Hindu in a letter to *The Times of India* (June 20, 1992) wrote: "It is wrong to say that the meaning of the Quranic verse where the word 'kill' is used, means to kill in reality. It means killing the habit of non-believing (in God)." A Hindu esoterist and synthesizer is quite capable of saying that the massacre of the Jews at Medina at the behest of the Prophet was an allegory and that what the Prophet meant was to "kill the Jew in the heart, that is one's own greed."

self-alienated, morally and ideologically disarmed. They lack leadership; the Hindu elites have become illiterate about their spiritual heritage and history and indifferent and even hostile towards their religion. In fact, they love every religion except their own.

Great poverty has overtaken Hindu religious institutions. Hindu temples are poor and in great neglect.[39] The functionaries connected with these institutions live in abject poverty and they are the poorest section in India.

The education of Hindus is not in their own hands; in fact, the teaching of Hinduism has been neglected for centuries and Hindu children grow in complete ignorance of their religion. Hinduism is becoming a non-practising and non-practised religion.

India's higher education, its academia and media are in the hands of a Hindu-hating elite. India's history is written by people under the influence of old Imperial schools. They tell you how Muslims and Christians came as liberators from the shackles of Hinduism.

Hindu society is badly divided. Once when Hinduism was strong, castes represented a natural and healthy diversity, but now in its present state of weakness these are used for its dismemberment. Old vested interests joined by new ones have come together to make use of the caste factor in a big way in

[39]Muslims had destroyed and looted the temples. The British did not do that but they took over a good deal of the temple lands as a 'revenue measure'; they did not use the word 'confiscation' and, in fact, converted some of these lands into 'monetary remuneration'. As a result, according to the Government of India's own comprehensive study beginning in 1962 and lasting for over ten years, the ten thousand five hundred and odd temples of Tamilnad have a total annual income of only rupees twenty-seven million, from all their moveable and immoveable properties! Over 5,000 temples have only an annual income of Rs.500/- each! There is almost no money for the pujas, and the priests also hardly get anything. The only people who get proper remunerations are the Government functionaries employed to overseer the working of the temples. The 14,000 priests in Madhya Pradesh got five naya paisa per month at the time of Independence; now they get six naya paisa according to the Madhya Pradesh Pujaris Mahasangh!

order to keep Hindus down.

Hindus have been kept down too long . Everyone including the victims think that it is the natural order of things. Therefore now when the Hindu society is showing some signs of stir, there is a great consternation. Already a cry has gone out of Hindu fundamentalism, we must expect more of it in future.

These are great odds but let us not dwell on them inordinately. Let us accept them in the spirit that God has sent them and their purpose must be good. Difficulties come in order to help. India has been asleep for long, and it needed all these knocks and probably it would get more. But let us hope that the difficulties would be overcome and Hinduism will come into its own and recover its self-nature and regain its natural pride, so that it can makes its contribution.

Reawakened Hinduism

When India rises again, many things will happen. During the long centuries of adversity Hindus of the sub-continent were under great pressure, and many of them were forced to leave their ancestral fold. But as Hinduism rises, they would like to come back home.

During its heyday, Hinduism had intimate cultural contacts with many countries of South East, Far East, Central and West Asia. But these contacts snapped during the preceding centuries when all of them came under very different pressures. A reawakened India will try to revive those contacts and re-establish old cultural links.

A reawakened India will also become aware of Africa and the Americas. During the last several centuries, she had no initiative in the matter; she knew others through Europe. But it need not be so now. She should now establish a direct contact with them and meet them on a deeper level of the spirit. She should discover traditional Africa and indigenous America for herself without Western-Christian or lately Marxist interpretation.[40] No doubt, we shall find a lot in common.

[40]In this connection, we reproduce two pieces as appendices. Appendix 2 gives the views of Nana (Queen) Boakyewa Yiadom I. She belongs to

During the last centuries, India had the closest relationship with Europe through England though, unfortunately, it was an unequal relationship. But some highly gifted and dedicated scholars were also at work and through their labour it was discovered that the links between the two peoples were very old indeed; that their languages derived from a common source, probably an old form of Sanskrit; that their speakers were also one people migrating from a common homeland probably in India; that they had also a common religion best represented by the Vedas, and shared common Gods close to Vedic Gods.[41]

The question becomes important now that many in Europe are seeking their old religious roots. Here the living Hindu tradition can help them. Opinions may differ about the true physical home of these people, but probably there might be agreement that 'Hinduism' or some form of Vedic religion is their 'spiritual' home.

The most important role that a reawakened Hinduism has to play is that of helping the world to understand its religious past.

Ghana and is a spokesperson of Africa's traditional religion, and of pan-African unity. The piece is reproduced from *Hinduism Today* (June, 1992). Appendix 3 is our own article, 'Indigenous America Waiting to be Rediscovered in a Hindu Way'. It is reproduced from *The Telegraph*, Calcutta, dated November 29, 1991.

[41]All this was obvious enough at the time even though it was not always put forward exactly in this form and in this language. Schlegel found India "the home of universal religion, the cradle of the noblest human race." J.C. Herder asked the question: "All the peoples of Europe, where are they from?" And he answered: "From Asia." Schopenhauer thought that India was the "fatherland of mankind," and he expressed the hope that European peoples "who stemmed from Asia... would re-attain the holy religions of their home." All this however changed under a growing consciousness of Imperial power and Euro-centricity. New theories reflected new power realities and new Imperial needs. Aryan dispersion from a common centre was retained, but its direction was changed and it became the theory of the Aryan invasion of India. The theory was meant to justify and to help the British Imperialism. The theory has little intellectual respectability left, but it has not lost its political usefulness and it is quite popular with the representatives of preceding Imperialisms and their Hindu apologists.

The reader further interested in the subject may refer to our article, 'Indo-European Encounter: An Indian Perspective', in *The Journal of Indian Council of Philosophical Research*, Vol. VIII, No. II, January–April, 1991.

Most countries have lost their old spiritual traditions, but Hinduism still retains them and it is a repository of spiritual knowledge that humanity has lost. Through awakened Hinduism, the whole past of religious humanity speaks as it were. Through it, one could still hear many old voices now lost or silenced.[42] Through it one could understand again Plato, Hermes Trismegistos, Apollonius, Plotinius. Through Vedanta alone Eckhart makes a deep sense, who otherwise remains incomprehensible if one depended on Christian tradition.

As we go further into humanity's past and study its great spiritual cultures, the need for Vedanta becomes still greater. There is no other way of understanding them except through a living culture which is also as ancient as they. Take Egypt, for example. We have happily found plenty of texts bearing on its religion, but the oral traditions through which its spiritual knowledge was transmitted was lost. Therefore, bare texts do not make a meaning as literalists have found. To understand them, "it is necessary that we turn to the Vedanta... because the *Upanishads* provide the purest metaphysics available to us from the primordial past," as Arthur Versluis, the author of *The Egyptian Mysteries*, says. He himself followed this method and he found that the study of Vedanta "in-fills" Egyptian studies. His labour resulted in an illuminating study of Egypt's ancient religious tradition.

[42]Let us remember that Christianity and Islam have taught their adherents to hold their past in contempt. They have also been great destroyers of cultures and spiritual traditions, sometimes even wiping out their very memory. For example, take Armenia's old religious literature. According to the *Encyclopaedia Britannica*, "Armenians had a temple literature of their own which was destroyed in the 4th and 5th centuries by Christian clergy so thoroughly that barely 20 lines of it survive [now] in the history of Moses of Khoren." They did the same to Egypt, Syria, Europe, the two Americas, and many parts of Asia. Islam did the same wherever it held sway. It completed Christianity's work in Egypt, Syria, Turkey; it destroyed the old cultures of Iran, Iraq and Central Asia. India managed to save itself from this fate. In the act of saving itself, it also saved many common cultural and spiritual traditions of the time. Hinduism has therefore a representative character and it holds the key to the understanding of many religious cultures of many countries.

The above discussion shows that Hinduism has a significant role to play in the world, but whether Indian Hindus are spiritually prepared for it is another matter. However, one thing is certain, that the rise of Hinduism will greatly help the rise of a spiritual humanity.

Appendix 1

EVANGELIZATION: THE GREAT COMMAND AND A COSMIC AUDITING*

The volume surveys 788 most important evangelizing Plans produced by Christianity during its career of over 19 hundred years. All these Plans relate to the Great Commission — the command that Jehovah gave through the mouth of His only Begotten Son, Jesus, to the believers to "go and make disciples of all nations" (Mt. 28.19, 20). If there was also a command to improve their morals, it was neglected, but the one to preach and recruit more followers for their God was rather taken in earnest. They promised Him to make "all the peoples of the earth know Him and fear Him" (2 Chr. 6.33).

The Survey is a statistical marvel, a worthy sequel to the *World Christian Encyclopaedia* (reviewed by us in *The Times of India*, July 14, 1985), by David Barrett, an outstanding statistician-evangelist and senior author of this volume under review. Quite in the spirit of the book, the two authors are introduced statistically as Missionaries who "have been involved in some 36 (10%) of all the 358 global plans between 1953 and 1988."

The book is divided into 4 parts and 28 chapters; it includes 10 Appendices, 27 Tables and Diagrams and a Bibliography, a selection of original and significant writings, classics, and other benchmark items on the subject of world evangelization.

The book does not include all the plans, but only a fraction of them representing merely "the tip of the iceberg." It however includes plans best known for their global significance and, as we approach modern times, most central plans of major Christian denominations or missions or parachurch agencies which each has over 5,000 foreign missionary personnel. The authors analyze these plans using 15 variables.

*A Review article of *Seven Hundred Plans to Evangelize the World: The Rise of a Global Evangelization Movement*, by David B. Barrett and James W. Reapsome. Pub: The AD 2000 Series. 1989. (Ram Swarup, *The Statesman*, Sunday Edition, March 25, 1990).

The biblical story that God created the world out of Chaos proves to the authors that He is a "God of order, of planning, of strategy." Similarly, the biblical observation that the "very hairs of your head are numbered" proves that God is also a great enumerator, and numberer. The authors do no more than imitate their God's skill and audit for us how His Great Commission has been followed by the believers.

Christianity has passed through 66 generations but for the best part of its life the Great Command has been neglected. "Disobeying the Great Commission: 59 Neglected Generations," has a separate chapter on it. During this while, there were only 2.6 plans per generation. But with the 19th century began the era of "five aware generations." During this time which also coincides with the heydays of Western Imperialism, the number of global plans per generation rose to 28. But the most "aware" and the richest in planning is the present century. During its first decade, the figure was 69 plans per generation, 321 during the 1970s, and the going rate is 1,200 global plans per generation.

In earlier centuries most global plans came from countries bordering on the Mediterranean. Then the shift took place to Europe, Russia and North America. Since AD 1900, the US alone has provided 247 global plans.

But while the plans have been abundant, their failures have been no less impressive. The book includes a chapter, "A Catalogue of Woes," which enumerates "340 reasons for 534 failed global plans." The reasons include such items as "ecclesiastical crime", "ecclesiastical gangsterism", "offering tempting inducements", the "use of laundered money", "mass religious espionage", "imperialism", "terrorism", etc.

Such reasons suggest as if these plans depended for their success on Christians being better than they were. But this is pure assumption. In fact, the reasons cited for their failure are often also reasons for their success. There could easily be a chapter on "X-number of reasons for successful Y-number of plans," and these would have rightly included imperialism, terrorism, coups, arrogance, etc. These indeed are cited when the authors discuss "Evolution of a global Evangelical movement" and name individually 304 years of evangelical significance. For example, they mention AD 323 for "attempts to spread gospel by law and authority" by Constantine; or cite C 780 for "forced baptism of Saxon race by Charlemagne, 4,500 executed in one day for resisting, thousands more deported"; or AD 1523, when the "Spanish monarch orders Cortes to enforce mass conversion of American Indians...in Mexico, Franciscans baptize over a million in 7 years, with at times 14,000 a day...C 1550, 800,00 Peruvian Amerindians confirmed by one archbishop of Lima."

Resources

Next to political power in importance are money and propaganda. The authors tell us about the resources at the command of Christian churches. They tell us that today it costs "145 billion dollars to operate organized global Christianity"; it commands 4.1 million full-time Christian workers, runs 13,000 major libraries, publishes 22,000 periodicals, issues 4 billion tracts a year, operates 1,800 Christian Radio/TV stations. We are also told that there are 3 million computers and the "Christian computer specialists" are described as "a new kind of Christian army."

Missionary activity is the major plank of organized Christianity. At present 4,000 Mission Agencies operate a huge apparatus of Christian world mission manned by 262,300 missionaries costing 8 billion dollars annually. Every year, there are 10,000 new books/articles on foreign evangelization alone. The authors give an interesting estimate and tell us that Christianity has expended on its missionary activities a "total of 160 million worker-years on earth over these 20 centuries." But since a missionary does not live by God alone, it has cost the church exchequer "somewhere in the neighbourhood of 350 billion dollars", or about 2,200 dollars per year per missionary.

From time to time special plans have also been drawn for evangelizing the world. On 788 of them surveyed here, 10 million worker-years and 45 billion dollars have already been expended. Right away there are 387 global plans at work and 254 of them are making progress. One hundred fifty-five of these plans are called "massive", defined as those which each expends "10,000 worker-years, or over 10 million dollars a year, for an average of 10 years." There are still bigger plans, 33 of them called gigantic, "gigaplan", "each with over 100,000 worker-years, or 100 million dollars a year, or a total of 1 billion dollars over the years of plan's life." The biggest current gigaplan is spending 550 million dollars a year on its missionary work.

We are told that though the church had "always had enormous resources," they did not always avail. Sometimes even well-endowed plans came to nothing. For example, in 1918, 336 million dollars were raised and then the plan was destroyed within a week. More recently, a gigaplan which raised 150 million dollars a year collapsed (did it?) in 1988 in a sex and management scandal which involved top evangelists. The reference is to Bakker and Jimmy Swaggart of the Assemblies of God.

Unreached people

But in spite of this massive effort, there are still "unreached people", places where the missionaries have not reached or where they have not succeeded. All these people have been "segmentized" into "bite-sized chunks" which number 3,000. They are placed under 5,000 missionaries of special calibre and training, well versed in research, logistics, briefing, monitoring, analyzing and coordinating, and modern communication techniques. Considering the nature of their work, they operate from places which are politically secure and which have modern facilities.

The greatest difficulty the missions are facing today is that they are being denied free run in many areas and face resistance from traditional religions or competing ideologies or nationalist sources. The authors say that uptil AD 1900, "virtually every country was open to foreign missionaries of one tradition or another," but at present "some 65 countries are closed...with three more closing their doors every year." But the missionaries have risen to the occasion and in order to overcome these difficulties, they operate a wide-spread underhand apparatus while their theorists propound new ways and try new strategies for penetrating these areas. That these methods involve moral and legal objections provides no deterrence. As the authors put it, in situations where their basic rights as Christian missionaries have been denied, they "have not hesitated to operate illegally, or secretly," as all history shows. The *Evangelical Missionaries Quarterly* justifies the subterfuge required of covert missionaries thus: "God does not lie, but he does keep secrets." Translated into the ethical code of his followers, this attribute of Jehovah means: Ask no questions and you will be told no lies.

Secret Apparatus

Missionaries to these areas or "target countries" are divided into various kinds: Tentmaker, Residential, Clandestine, Mole, Tourist, Courier, Smuggler and Non-residential. Each category has a defined status and role. Advantage is taken of the fact that even a country most restrictive of missionaries maintains a variety of contacts with the West—commercial, diplomatic, technical, tourist. Thus men are sent out to these semi-closed countries who openly work in a secular job as technicians, diplomats or social workers but also secretly belong to a missionary agency. Such men are called Tentmakers *a la* St. Paul, who earned his bread by tentmaking but voluntarily worked as a missionary. This channel is highly organized. For example, *Tentmakers International*, Seattle, Washington, a Missionary body, runs a "tentmaker placement network", working closely with private and social agencies. It has a list of 15,000 secular jobs for which it recruits *tentmakers*. "Jobs are available worldwide. Choose your country, take your pick," it advertises. Then everything becomes secretive. A warning is issued: "Please use commonsense when talking about *Tentmakers International*. Confidentiality is a must."

The Clandestine is a "full-time missionary who operates illegally." In the restricted countries, "much ministry is carried in this way," the authors tell us. The *Mole*, a word used in certain Intelligence Services, is another such type. He is a "part-time Christian worker, an illegal residential alien." A *Courier* is a "visitor from abroad who illegally carries messages to, from, and between local Christians and *Clandestine* workers." *Tourists* also come handy for this purpose. Every year more than 100 million Christian foreigners enter those restricted countries, and hundreds of them "are persuaded to act as couriers by Western Agencies," the authors tell us. Another category is *Smuggler*, a "full-time professional and seasoned Christian worker who operates illegally as an itinerant." One of the most famous of them is Brother Andre author of the best-seller, *God's Smuggler*.

These foreign types have their local counterparts which include categories like *Unregistered, Undergrounder, Messenger, Guerrilla*. For example, an *Undergrounder* is the citizen equivalent of the foreign *Mole*, a *Messenger* of the alien *Courier*. "Huge underground evangelizing networks exist operated by messengers utilizing solely word of mouth — no letters, no writing, no telephone," the authors reveal. They also tell us that "around the world are many thousand Guerrillas," a category parallel to foreign *Smugglers*.

These two groups of aliens and citizens work in unison. To illustrate, the authors cite the example of the "Pearl Operation" of 1981. In this Operation, 200 tons of Bible, one million volumes in all, were landed illegally at night off Swatow, China, and all quickly taken away by some 20,000 Chinese Christians. We are told that the "Operation was masterminded by alien *Smugglers* and citizen *Guerrillas*, using a complex network of foreign *Couriers*, citizen *Messengers*, and *Clandestine* workers from different countries to alert thousands of ordinary Chinese Christians, large number of *Unregistered* pastors, and other part-time *Undergrounders* and *Moles*."

Martyrs

Sometimes these underhand workers are apprehended and punished; then they join the roaster of *Martyrs*, who currently number 230,000 a year according to our authors.

Two such *Moles* or *Smugglers* were apprehended in Nepal in December, 1988. They were Mervyn Budd, 22, a Canadian, and McBride, 33, an American, both working for a US-based

Missionary organization, called "Operation Mobilization." As soon as the news of their arrest was splashed over the world, other sentiments and forces came into play. People forgot to inquire who these two men were and only remembered that they had their "civil" rights. Jack Anderson wrote in his weekly column: "Imagine being thrown in jail for selling religious literature," making McBride's activity as innocent as that. He told us how American Congressmen like Robert Walker and Senators Richard Lugar and Clairborne Pell took an active interest and "put pressure on the Nepalese Government." Amnesty International too was active.

Weak and poor countries of the third world have hardly any chance against these pressures and tactics. While the UNO recognizes the right of the Missionaries to operate their highly-endowed and subversive apparatus, it offers the weak countries no protection against it.

Cosmic Auditing

The authors give us some very interesting figures. They have no use for the traditional biblical chronology which allows man a bare 4,000 years of sojourn on the earth (according to a 17th century computations, man appeared on the earth on October 23 of BC 4004 and the apostles were already getting ready for the end of the world in their times). Our authors however take a long stride, back and forth, and go back to 5.5 million years when Homo appeared on the scene and they traverse 4 billion years in future. Undeterred by the fact that the new perspective involves grave theological problems, they boldly audit for us the missionary activity for all this era.

By the time Jesus came, 5.5 million years had already elapsed and 118 billion men and women had already lived and died, all *ipso facto* destined for hell as they did not know Christ. But new prospects opened for mankind after AD 33 when the Kingdom of Heaven was announced and inaugurated. Heaven, empty uptil then, began to be populated though rather unexpectedly slowly in the beginning. But by 1990, there are already 8 billion *dead* believers (Church Triumphant), all qualifying for habitation in the new region. They are however still only 5.70% of unbelievers destined for hell, quarters across the street. But the demographic composition continues to improve in their favour. By AD 2100, they are 8.57%, and at the end of 4 billion years, they are fully 99.90%, the Christian heaven holding 9 decillion (one decillion is ten followed by 33 zeros) believers.

In AD 100,000, believers are still only 85% of the total living population. But by AD 4 billion, the gap practically closes and almost all are believers. The Great Commission is fulfilled and Missionaries are freed from their obligation to God and His Son.

The population figures given here take into account men whose longevity after AD 2,500 turns gradually into immortality, and new men and human species artificially created by mass cloning and genetic engineering (Missionaries of the future believing, brave new world will have a different role; they will increasingly be able to raise their own crop of believers through genetic technology); they take into account humans increasingly living on off-earth space colonies, then across other galaxies and universes. In AD 4 billion, the "ultimate size of the Church of Jesus Christ," the authors estimate, will be "1 decillion believers," not counting 9 decillion dead by then.

This is indeed a cosmic auditing of the evangelical movement. David Barrett is a fitting Consultant on World Evangelism to the Vatican and to the Southern Baptist Foreign Mission Board, but one wonders whether these figures would excite them or depress them and whether they would know what to do with them. Figures and planning of this scale cease to be meaningful.

The Survey is eminent in statistics but poor in philosophy and spiritual wisdom. In fact, its psychic source is crass materialism.

APPENDIX 2

WE BELIEVE THAT THE EARTH IS GOD'S GIFT TO US*

There is a strong revival of African traditional religion going on at this time, and the African is notoriously religious. The key to understanding him is through his religion. He considers God as our universal Father. For the Akans of Ghana, He is also our divine Mother, *Nyame Obaatan Pa,* a very caring provider. God is omnipotent, *Gye Nyame,* all-knowing, omnipresent and sustainer of the whole world. In African culture, all revolves around religion which strongly influences the living and thinking of the ordinary man and woman. In fact, African religion, no matter the level of sophistication or education of the individual, permeates every aspect of his life, from seedtime to harvest, through the rites of passage, birth, puberty, marriage, death and hereafter. We have no creeds to recite, as these dwell in the heart, and each one is himself the living creed.

All over Africa, the earth is regarded as the female spirit *Asase Yaa,* Mother Earth. One is expected to care for her, nurse, cherish and love her. Generally, one will not till the land without her prior permission. We ask her permission again before digging to bury the dead so that her child may return into her womb. Thursday is set aside for her, and on that day many Akans will not till the land. Asase Yaa is also known as the upholder of truth, and whenever someone's word is in doubt, he is asked to touch his lip to some soil to become credible.

Before every function and ceremony, a libation is done whereby water or spirit are poured onto the ground while calling the name of God, Mother Earth and the ancestors, and beseeching their blessings upon all present. Some have criticized this practice, but that is because they do not understand that every single act or gesture of an Akan has a significance. Gesture and

*Article by Queen Boakyewa Yiadom I, reproduced from *Hinduism Today,* August, 1992

symbol play an important part in African rites. When in a dance a priestess raises her hands, she is delivering a message, "I am leaving all in the power of God."

We do not worship ancestors, but they are honored and revered as spirits and elders who stand close to God, who are a link between the living and the dead.

The European missionaries who colonized Africa from 1900 to 1945 condemned everything African — the religion, art, music and the systems of names, inheritance and marriage. Africans were forced to abandon their culture and adopt the Western style of life.

However, colonialism was mostly an urban phenomenon; it did not penetrate the rural areas where the majority lived. There, the tradition survived. It is still the way of life today and has tremendous influence on most Africans, whether Christian or Muslim [but what are Christianity and Islam doing there — author]. Almost all faithfully carry out the rites of passage. Children are given indigenous names, and the naming and *outdooring* (first-outing) ceremonies for babies, as well as puberty rites, traditional marriage and funeral rites all are done before their Western counterparts.

The aim of African religion is to promote harmony between man, the spirit world, society and the environment. Its distinctive feature is the sharing spirit. We believe that the earth is God's gift to us. We are merely the keepers of the earth and are charged with taking care of it and leaving it in a better condition than we found it. If we fail, our children will not have any earth to inherit.

Appendix 3

INDIGENOUS AMERICA WAITING TO BE REDISCOVERED IN A HINDU WAY*

On 12th October, 1986, the USA organised a festival to celebrate Columbus's discovery of the New World. The Statue of Liberty, the guardian of the New York harbour, was symbolically married to the 170-feet high statue of Columbus in Barcelona. Mr. Edward Koch, the Mayor of New York, acted as the proud father of the bride, Miss Liberty.

But one wonders if this could also be a day of jubilation for the native Indian Americans who in so far as they survived general extermination were made into hewers of wood and drawers of water in their own homes. Five hundred years ago, on this day, they fell under an evil star and a process began in which they lost their hearths and homes, their land, their liberties, their language and culture, their Gods and religion and their wonted way of life. Their funeral became the newcomers' festivity. I could not help recalling a book which I read recently: *The Inconstant Savage* by H.C. Porter, published by Duckworth in 1979.

Columbus landed on the American soil on 12th October. Within three days of his landing, he noted that the natives had "quick intelligence" and would make "good servants". But his adventure was not all for gold and political domination. He was also a faithful soldier of the Church and on the fifth day, on the 16th, he also noted of the natives that "no creed is known to them, and I believe that they would be speedily converted to Christianity". His biographical accounts tell us that wherever he went, it was his custom to set up a cross as "an emblem of Christ Jesus our Lord, and to the honour of Christendom".

The struggle was unequal. The newcomers had arms, horses, wheeled carriages and dogs; the natives had only their bare

*Article by Ram Swarup, reproduced from *The Telegraph*, Calcutta, dated November 29, 1991.

bodies — though as Gonzalo Fernandez Oviedo, a naturalist, observed the bones of their foreheads were "four times thicker" and so many swords were "broken on their heads with little harm done." Soon many of them were organised into *Encomienda*, a form of economic organisation by which the natives were made into slaves on land which in legal fiction still belonged to them. Culturally, there was the notorious "Requerimienta", which required the natives to embrace the Faith and to submit to the authority of the Pope and the rulers of Castile (Pope Alexander's Bull of May 1493), which if they failed to do, empowered the Spaniards to seize their lands and goods and to enslave their persons.

The colonization and its methods did not go undebated. But with rare exceptions, the ethics and theology were all on the side of the colonizers. One Juan Gines de Sepulvada, a theoretician and theologian, argued that wars against the American Indians were "very just", that the Indians were bound to submit to the Spaniards "as the foolish to the wise." It was also argued that the Indians were "idolators", an important point to make because it meant that it was quite in order and even righteous to make them slaves. Luke was also quoted: Go out to the highways and hedges, and compel people to come in, that my house may be filled — a favourite biblical text for forced conversions and for the suppression of heretics ever since St. Augustine used it in support of this purpose.

A hundred years elapse and the same drama is enacted in the North; the main characters in the drama are the British, the French and the unfortunate Red Indians. Again, God's hand is seen in the selection of the locale and the actors. Edward Hayes, Captain and owner of a ship, 'Golden Hind', that sailed to St. John's Newfoundland, assures us that God had appointed the limits of the Spaniards "not to exceed North of Florida" and that He "had reserved the countries to be by us converted unto the faith at His appointed time."

Today's intellectual fashion emphasizes economic and political motivation, but to the first colonizers religious motive was highly important. Robert Johnson, a future Deputy Director of the Virginia Company, urged in 1609 that the first concern of the Virginia settlement should be "to advance and spread the Kingdom of God, and the knowledge of his truth, among so many millions of men and women, savage and blind, that never yet saw the true light".

William Crashew, an ordained Calvinist minister, made a similar exhortation in his Virginia Company sermon. He said that while the settlers made their twenty percent, they should not be forgetful "of converting ten thousand souls to God". He added: "Remember the end of this voyage is the destruction of the Devil's Kingdom, and propagation of the gospel."

All this was possible because as Edward Hayes (mentioned above) had already found out in 1583 that the natives were "destitute of edge-tools and weapons, whereby they shall be unable to defend themselves or to offend us." Missionary zeal, finding no check, became more righteous and ran riot. The results were disastrous for the cultures and religions of the people of the two Americas. *Hinduism Today* (Nov.–Dec., 1986 Issue) provides a telling example in Hawaiin people who "numbered nearly 500,000 a century ago, are now less than 50,000 — their culture gone, their language spoken by a mere 500 people and their Gods worshipped by a dying handful of *kahuna* priests."

This is all about the past of these unfortunate people but what about their future? There are signs that they may rise again, phoenix-like, from their ashes. Their "medicine men" are beginning to speak. They are discovering that their old religion was deep, that it did not believe that man was conceived in sin but held there is only one Great Spirit and one Great Mystery which is seen all around — Is this the *sarvam khalvidam brahma* (verily, the whole world is Brahma) of the Hindus? Their religion believed in the great balance in nature and the great law of harmony (the *rita* of the Vedas).

While the Missionaries sang the familar missionary song, "Lost in the dark the heathen doth languish", the old racial type is coming to the fore. In the North, the old stock is pretty exterminated, but in many other countries of the Central and Southern Americas, people are "growing dark", a new racial reassertion is taking place at the biological level. Will it also lead to cultural and religious reassertion? Will the people go back to their roots and rediscover themselves? Racial reassertion will have no great significance without cultural reassertion. The latter alone will make a contribution to the world's spiritual store.

Remember that America was discovered during Europe's search for India. Is it all chance, or does it have some deeper meaning on another plane? Are the two peoples of the two antipodal lands interlinked in some invisible way? Indians should learn to take a deeper interest in American Indians. Is not the Great Spirit of the American Indians the same as the *Brahma* of the Hindus, the *purusham mahāntam* of the Upanishads? America is waiting to be rediscovered in a characteristically Hindu way, not the Christian way.

INDEX